"Rob 38:43 – It's a bible like philoso belief. Sales is a key part of what we do in keeping the bad habits at bay."

Nick Rundle, Insight Business & Financial Services.

"What I like most was being taken out of my comfort zone and being shown how easy it is to get your clients saying 'yes'. Rob is confident and speaks from experience – it all ties in together at the end. It makes the complicated seem simple."

Jason Fagg, Capricorn Investment Partners Limited

"Rob Nixon…..Energy, enthusiasm with an absolute belief that we can do it, great opportunity to learn."

Alan Bliss, Partner, The Practice

"Rob has given me the tools and knowledge to grow myself and the business."

Hamish Pryde, Coombe Smith

"I enjoyed learning new material and Rob's ability to make every scenario simple and straight forward forcing attendees to leave the 'fluff' out of servicing clients at the door. Love Rob's 'take no crap' approach!"

Kelli Willmer, Hern Financial Services

"Rob, you truly get full team participation to happen. We discovered how to maximize our potential. Team buy-in is what is needed and Rob is great at fostering this."

Sean Loader, Business Manager, HAS Business Solutions

"Prior to joining we were already a successful firm. Rob and Coaching Club were instrumental in helping us improve our net profit by 61% in two years. Our first focus in Coaching Club was on increasing our efficiency or getting our back yard in order. We achieved immediate results by implementing a number of simple strategies. However our big gains were achieved through value pricing. Rob constantly reminded us of the Intellectual Property that we had developed over a number of years and the need to put an appropriate value on it. The discipline and accountability involved in Coaching Club, along with the interaction with our peers helped us to take our business to a much higher level."

Greg Brennan, Partner – Brennan Sloan Leahy

"We have been working with Rob Nixon since February 2006 at which time our business had a turnover of approximately $7m. During this time we have completely restructured the way over business operates from a services and resourcing perspective. We are now fully operating in a less paper environment with excellent management reporting systems. Having thrown away charge rates our staff are committed to achieving the best results they can for both the client and ourselves.

The business is now in a very organised position. With a concise business plan in place and action plans specifically focused on achieving these goals we will see our business grow to 4 times its original size but with a vastly improved efficiency.

The coaching environment has been crucial in changing our mindsets and focusing our attention on implementing those strategies that truly allow us to deliver an unparalleled client experience.

We would not have taken our business to this level without the support of Rob and his team."

David Carpenter, Partner, Cutcher & Neale

"WOW - In our supercharge day with Rob we were delivered energy, passion, inspiration and ideas to make things really happen in our business. The team now have the confidence to know that there are no boundaries and anything is possible in our business."

Chris Mandzufas, Brentnalls

"I have more ideas and tactics to implement in educating my people and clients, therefore generating more successful leads. I have real tried and tested tools such as the lockdown script to improve customer service. The workshop has enabled me to see the opportunity in learning business skills that apply outside Accounting and personal skills that empower me to be my best. I could go on forever, Rob and his team are outstanding people. Genuinely motivating, inspiring and backed up facts with results."

Karissa Clare, Simeoni & Co

"Coaching Club has changed us from accountants to businessmen and turned our firm from a practice to a business"

Eddie Taylor, Shearer + Elliss

ACCOUNTING PRACTICES PRACTICES DON'T ADD UP!

Why they don't and what to do about it

Rob Nixon

© Copyright 2011 Rob Nixon
ISBN: 978-1-921787-35-5
Published by VIVID Publishing
P.O. Box 948, Fremantle
Western Australia 6959
www.vividpublishing.com.au
2nd edition - International.

To my loving wife Natalie and awesome children, Hugh, Oliver and Harriet. Your love and support has enabled me to do what I do best - help accounting firms achieve massive success. For all the time I have been away, for all the late nights I have been out with clients and the crazy hours that I keep a BIG thank you for keeping 'the home fires burning', being there for me and understanding my passion. Without your love, support and enthusiasm - I could not do what I do. I love you all.

Contents

About the Author

Rob Nixon is not an accountant. Yet he has forged a niche to be the world's foremost authority on how accounting firms can achieve peak performance.

He is an entrepreneur who has been running successful businesses since 1986. Since 1994 he has been running businesses that specialise in helping accountants run better, more profitable businesses.

Accountants intrigue Rob and over the years he has trained them, consulted to them, coached them, researched them and visited thousands of them. All in the pursuit of what works and what does not work.

His speaking work has taken him all over the world where he has spoken to in excess of 70,000 accountants. Currently his monthly newsletter 'proactive' is distributed to accountants in 27 countries. The training products he has created are used extensively by over 16,000 accountants and his landmark ideas and strategies are adopted by large and small firms all over the world.

His biggest achievement is the creation of the revolutionary coaching model called coachingclub. The coachingclub model enables firms to be accountable, to consistently learn and to share ideas amongst their peers. The model is so successful that on average the coachingclub members are 93% more profitable than the rest of the profession. Rob is a keen golfer, adventurer and runner. He lives in sunny Brisbane, Australia with his lovely wife Natalie and 3 children.

Introduction

Since May 1994 I have been working exclusively with accountants and accounting firms. Helping them to grow and develop themselves. I am not an accountant (in fact I finished school when I was just 16) and that gives me a distinct advantage. I tend to look at things a bit differently and I offer a perspective from a 'real world' business point of view.

There was no grand plan to start working with accountants. I literally 'fell' into the accounting profession. Here's how it happened.

I was running a series of customer service seminars in 1994 (I was 24 at the time) and an accountant (Ellis) attended one of my (very small) seminars. He said, 'Will you come to my town and do this seminar for my clients?' He worked in a small country town called Coonamble in NSW Australia - population 2,500. He told me he had 126 clients.

Never one to miss an opportunity I jumped at the chance to apply one of my favourite marketing strategies – host beneficiary marketing. He promoted the event to his clients using my marketing materials and 56 people turned up to the Coonamble RSL club. I made a profit of $2,500 on the night (the most ever at the time) and he did a great thing for his client base and the community. It was the largest event I had ever done and the first one that made a profit! I realised right away that accountants had marketing leverage because of their trusted advisor status and loyalty in their client base. So I immediately stopped all of the other marketing activities (mail, fax, radio, print advertising and T.V.) that were sending me broke and decided to concentrate 100% on accountants.

Initially my seminars were for the accountants' clients then I started working directly with firms on a training and consulting basis. I moved on to providing benchmarking services, then knowledge management software and since November 2005 creating a proactive network of accountants who adopt my principals through my unique coaching model 'The Accountants coachingclub'.

I am now entering my 18th year working exclusively with accountants (from the micro businesses to the multi- nationals) and I travel the world (they do the same things everywhere) speaking, coaching and consulting. I train accountants in all facets of business improvement, researching, benchmarking and creating tools and products., I have written countless articles on my findings and I have created companies that serve accountants.

Anyone would think I like accountants. I do!

I even have a running shirt that says on the front of it:

I

Accountants

People look at me strangely when I wear that shirt.

The way I work is by observation. I visit firms; I observe what they are doing and speak with them on a daily basis to see what is working and what is not. I take the best bits from each firm, add my twists and insights and then recreate it for the entire profession.

This book really is a book of 'best practice'. It is a detailed summary of what I have learned over the years on what works and what does not. My promise is that if you apply these ideas, tactics and strategies you will run a better business and in turn you will enjoy your professional and personal life more than you ever thought possible.

Enjoy the ride!

Rob Nixon
Brisbane, Australia, February 2011

1

What's Right and Wrong with the Traditional Model

I am convinced that the inventors of the current profit model of an accounting practice were <u>not</u> very good at strategy or business development. I am certain that the creators of this model had charity in mind. I am also convinced that the current model will bring in a decent income (and maybe a reasonable lifestyle if you are frugal) but it will not make you wealthy.

Now that I have your attention let me share with you what is right and wrong with the traditional model.

The Bizarre Habits

The current model just does not add up – it's flawed from the start. Take a look at how the vast majority of accounting practices around the world make a profit.

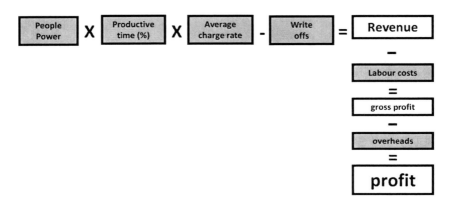

Most partners of most accounting practices earn $200K - $400K per annum. However, that's before taxation and working capital. You can build a reasonable lifestyle but it won't make you wealthy!

This model truly is bizarre. The success of the revenue model is predicated on…

1. A volume of people to do the work – who always seem to be in short supply.

2. Squeezing maximum chargeable hours out of the accounting team. (In a Scottish accent the partners rant, "We want more billable hours out of you laddy.")

3. Increasing charge rates. However they are typically linked to salary levels so you get marginal profit improvement.

4. Reducing write-offs, which is discounting before billing. While you price in arrears you will never ethically reduce write-offs.

5. Reducing labour costs. Since when has that strategy worked?

6. Reducing overheads and being extremely frugal. See point above!

What wrong with all that, you say?

The entire model is based on 'labour for hire' and that is not what you sell. You sell what you know; you sell intellectual capital turned into intellectual property, which is disguised as letters, reports, statements of advice, meetings and recommendations. You DO NOT sell labour – yet that is what your business model says you sell.

Around the world at various partner retreats (why they are called a retreat is beyond me – I thought you were supposed to be 'advancing' at these things – not 'retreating') I am sure at pontification time the following discussions have taken place…

Partner A:

"If we could only find another 5 qualified Accountants and get 1250 hours out of each of them at an average charge rate of $200 net of 10% write offs then we can grow our revenue by $1.25M."

Partner B:

"Or another way to do this is to try to squeeze more productivity out of our current 15 accountants, from 1200 hours to 1400 hours and increase their charge rates from an average of $150 to $165. That would increase our profit by $45,000."

Partner C:

"I think we need to reduce our write-offs from 15% down to 5%. We have been targeting 15% for years – why don't we target 5% write-offs?

We have been writing off $300,000 and the new target would only be $100,000."

Partner D:

"But what about our labour and overhead costs? We were planning to give the team a 5% pay increase this year – one of them even asked me for 20% for goodness sake – why don't we just give them a 3% increase. Our IT costs are out of control, I think if we spend some time re-negotiating our contract we could save at least $15,000 per annum."

What is wrong with the discussion?

- ☒ Increasing the head count – labour costs and general overheads just went up as well.
- ☒ Squeezing chargeable time – just go slower and make more mistakes, that will increase chargeable time.
- ☒ Increasing charge rates – the team will expect to be paid more.
- ☒ Still budgeting for write-offs – what a strategy that is.
- ☒ Paying people less than they are worth – well that's going to work.
- ☒ Spending an inordinate amount of time scrutinizing reducing expenses for little return.

Write-offs

Another bizarre habit that accountants get involved in is 'writing-off'. Write-offs (discounting before billing) occur in 3 distinct areas:

1. At the time of setting the annual budget. Line 1 on the budget says, 'Expected fees charged to WIP (work in progress).' Line 2 says, 'Expected write-offs'. How bizarre, expecting to fail

before you start. *I visited a six-partner firm in Melbourne once. They had fees charged to WIP of $9.7M and write-offs of $2.6M. Net fees billed of $7.1M. They wrote-off nearly 27% or another way to look at it they set fire to a luxury home every year – and that would have been more enjoyable. Anyway, I asked the 6 partners if they budgeted for write-offs. Yes we do they said. What's your budgeted number? 25% they proudly stated. I said, 'Well you nearly hit it.'* Bizarre behaviour – budgeting for write-offs. What would happen if you budgeted for write-ons? You might hit it.

2. The other time write-offs occur is at the time of doing the work. In workshops, I ask accountants to honestly answer how much time they put on the clock whilst doing the work. The accountants in question all use an archaic method of time-based billing in arrears, which that what goes on the clock multiplied by the charge rate should be billed to clients. How much time hits the clock? The average is 85%. A staggering 15% of the time taken does not hit the clock in the first place. The gutless partners do not even have a chance to write it off.

3. The most obvious area where write-offs occur is at the time of billing. With all the pride in the world the accountant who did the work presents it to the (typically) partner for review and to determine the size of the bill that the client will receive. The partner looks at the work and says, 'The client will never pay that,' and promptly wipes off 5,10,15 or 20% of the value of the project.

So if you budget for write-offs expect to get them. If you use time and rate as your billing method expect to get them and if you have gutless partners at the time of billing expect to get them. You get what you expect.

Pricing Methods

A client comes to you for business advice. The client specifically wants some ideas on how much they should charge their customers for a new product. With as much sage advice as you can muster you say, *"What you should do is work out how much time it will take to make the product. Then work out a charge rate for each person who is making the product. You work out the charge rate by taking the annual salary and dividing by the time they are at work for the year – say 1687 hours – then multiply that number by 4 times and you have a charge rate. Multiply the time taken by the charge rate and you have the price for the product. That's what we do here and it has worked for decades."*

Your client says, "I haven't made the product yet." It doesn't matter you say, *"Follow the magic formula and it will lead you to the correct price."*

Or what about this way to set a price:

Let's say (gentleman) you want to buy a suit. You go to your favourite tailor on Saville Row in London. You enter the shop and the following dialogue takes place:

You: "How much for a suit?"

Tailor: "That depends."

You: "Depends on what?"

Tailor: "It depends on the type of fabric I use to make the suit."

You: "Ok, I'll select that one there – how much for the suit?"

Tailor: "That depends."

You: "Depends on what?"

Tailor: "It depends on how much of the fabric we use for your suit (under breath – fatso)."

You:	"Ok measure me up – I'm a 42 inch chest and a 30" waist (yeah right)."
You:	"Now how much for the suit?"
Tailor:	"That depends."
You:	(Getting frustrated) "Depends on what?"
Tailor:	"It depends on the quality of the thread, volume of buttons and patches that we use."
You:	"Ok, I'll go with these ones. Right then, now how much for the suit?"
Tailor:	"That depends."
You:	(Getting mad now) "Depends on what?"
Tailor:	"Well it depends on how much time it takes me to make it for you."
You:	"You mean to tell me that the longer you take the more I will have to pay?"
Tailor:	"Precisely, Sir."

And that is how accounting practices work out the price. Time X Rate + Disbursements. That is no way to price a product.

Bizarre behaviour. The only way to set a price is to have the market place (clients) set the price. You just test different packaging and price every project up front. The price for intellectual property is based on just 2 factors:

1. Your personal value belief.
2. Your clients value perception.

You will know that the price is wrong when your client says yes, without hesitation. If your clients keep saying YES then the price is WRONG.

Partner Habits

As I mentioned, since May 1994 I have been working exclusively with accounting firms and I am constantly bemused at what the owners (partners) of the firms do with their time. If I visit a 4-partner firm, I will ask their roles:

The first partner says, "I am the marketing partner."

The second one says, "I am the IT partner."

The third one says, "I am the HR partner."

And the fourth one so proudly says, "And I am the operations partner."

Yet not one of them know 'diddly squat' (technical term for very little) about these 4 important topics. Have a look at how partners (you) spend their time. Keep a time log of everything you do. When the time log starts to repeat itself, stop keeping the log. Go back over the list and work out the 'highest dollar productive activity' that you do and highlight that one. Then work out the 2nd and 3rd highest dollar productive activity. Get rid of the rest. They'll mainly be administration tasks. Delegate them, don't do them and get focused on 3 only.

Partners should only be doing 3 key things:

1. High-end chargeable work (advisory, cash flow, profit improvement, structuring type work) for the percentage of time that keeps you interested. No charge rates with this sort of work – all value based fees.

2. Building relationships with existing clients. Visiting them, phoning them up and getting to know them – finding out what they need and then selling additional services to them.

3. Leadership. Driving performance of the business, searching for new ideas. New products to sell, new clients.

Everything else is administration. Hire a business manager to do it – not you.

Partners' meetings can be interesting and bizarre things to watch. As well as looking over the previous month's numbers and chastising whatever under-performance needs chastising they get into discussions on costs and petty details. I have seen partners debate (kid you not) what colour the receptionist's chair needs to be and which model to select for him/her. *"I saw a chair which would be perfect at the wholesale office store for $99. It was $23 cheaper than where we normally buy chairs."* Majoring on the minors and management by committee. Bizarre. Can someone (not the committee) please make a decision. Empower people and trust them.

Also at partners meetings the topic of marketing may come up (by the marketing partner no less) and there may be a seminar to invite clients to. "None of my clients will be interested," says one of the partners. "I think I have 5 or 6 only that may want to go," says another.

I have even met partners who debate if they should send the electronic newsletter to some clients. "They'll never read it." How bizarre. Pre-judging what clients will buy, how they will act, what they will respond to and what they are interested in. I think pre-judging has to be one of the most arrogant activities around. For the sake of your clients stop pre-judging. Let your clients know about everything you do and see who responds. Simple.

I remember a 3 partner firm joined one of my coachingclub programs (group coaching method that creates outstanding results – when the clients follow the advice) and their lockup (Work in progress 'WIP' and Debtors combined) was *running at around $900K. For a $2M firm this was out of control. There was around $750K in WIP and $150K in debtors. By the time we met again the WIP balance was down $50K and debtors were around $125K. Good result I said – how did you do it? Answer – one of the partners decided to write off $650K! I hit the roof. Before even giving it a chance to be collected it was written off. I hasten to say, that partnership no longer exists. Bizarre behaviour.*

What bizarre behaviour exists in your firm? I would love to hear your story. Send me an email with your story – rob@robnixon.com. If you wish, I'll protect your privacy and keep your story anonymous.

Order Takers and History Writers

Unbeknownst to those who work in accounting practices, the favourite word (and often it seems the firm's mantra and culture) is to '**wait**'. Here is some dialogue you may have heard before.

Q. "Why can't we get that job out?"

A. "I have sent the client an email and I am now waiting for them to send the missing bank statement in."

Q. "Why is your productivity so low?"

A. "I was waiting for the graduate to finish his/her part of the work."

Q. "When can we grow the revenue?"

A. "We'll have to wait until the government changes the rules and we can then write to our clients and tell them we need to do …."

Q. "Why haven't we sold more budget and cash flow forecasts?"

A. "We've been waiting for the banks to tell the clients that they need one."

Q. "What have you been doing all day?"

A. "I have been waiting for the phone to ring, the email to ping, the client to come in and the team member to complain about being paid so poorly."

Reactive Accountants **wait, wait and wait**.

It was once said that some people make things happen, some people wait for things to happen and some people wonder what happened. Which one are you? What is the culture of your firm?

This waiting mentality creates 'order taker' mentality. Constantly on the back foot, dealing with client issues (putting out fires), and never getting on the front foot and being proactive.

Clients want you to be proactive. They do not know what they do not know. They want advice. They want help. They want someone to tell them what to do.

Among other things, you are the expert on finance, cash flow management and structuring – not your client. If you see an opportunity where your client could use your services then you owe it to them to tell them. If you do not promote all of your services then you are doing your clients a complete disservice.

If you continue down the 'order taker' route for compliance then you are basically a history writer. Primarily writing up the past. If you continue down this track then you will be a slave to the government and a post office for the taxation department.

Do your clients want you to be a history writer who waits for history to happen? I think not. Do *you* want to be a history writer?

By way of actions, many accountants say yes, that's it – history writing and waiting is for me.

They assume that they know what the client wants so they just give them what they ask for. Accountants constantly prejudge what the clients want and never give them what they really need. As I said earlier, I think prejudging is one of the most arrogant actions possible.

No doubt you've heard the term – ready, aim, and fire. The challenge with the accountants' mentality is that without coaching you will spend most of the time 'getting ready'. Most accountants spend their whole life getting 'ready' (the spreadsheet or the system will never be right), they rarely aim and hardly every fire.

By getting ready they WAIT. You have a disclaimer on everything (I suppose that means you don't even think the numbers are right) so what have you got to lose. Start aiming and start firing.

Instead of waiting to write up your clients' history...**help them to make history.**

Steady as She Goes

The traditional growth model is a slow and steady path to moderate success. Most years an accounting firm grows by revenue. It's a simple equation. Put the charge rates up each year (unfortunately salaries go up as well), accept a few new clients by referral, retain the clients you already have and voila, the revenue increases.

But does the profit increase? Typically not.

This reactive 'steady as she goes' approach causes 2 critical issues that hold back the performance of the firm – and ultimately your clients being delighted to deal with you.

1. **Apathy**
2. **Self esteem**

It is relatively easy to make money in an Accounting Practice. Seriously, you do not have to try that hard to make a decent profit. You know that around 90% of revenue will come in each year. You can write the budget on the 90%. It's effectively recurring revenue – you know it's there you just have to bring in the work. You know that the government will change the rules and you'll need to introduce something new to your clients. You know that some of your clients will get in financial trouble and you'll need to help them out with a re-finance or similar. You know you can get away with paying your people 50% - 100% less than they are worth because everyone does that. You know that you will get some new clients by referral – not many but there will be some.

This reactive, steady as she goes approach is comfortable. However, this comfort zone breeds **apathy,** it creates laziness and you start to believe that all you are going to get it all you are going to get. Your dreams and aspirations all but disappear. And because your life is all about reacting all day every day your **self esteem declines**. You start to talk a lot in client meetings, you constantly give the answer to clients in detail (and quickly) and you write long arduous and verbose letters, statements of advice and invoices. You do not listen attentively to people and you start being a bully to others – all are sure-fire signs of low self-esteem.

You are strong when the client comes to you but not so strong when you go to the client with an idea.

If the 'steady as she goes' approach breeds apathy and low self-esteem then the knock-on effect is that you do not help your clients fully and you do not reach your business potential.

You end up with minimal business value, minimal assets or savings in your superannuation or pension program, and you settle for less than you should at retirement.

I want for you to have a BIG problem. I want you to have a high self-esteem problem. I want for you to enjoy the life you deserve and I want for you to realise your business and personal potential.

To do that you MUST do something different. Your decisions and actions of the past got you the results you achieve today.

Another way to look at this is that you are where you are because you choose to be!

Will the same strategies of the past realise your success of tomorrow?

Do Clients Want More?

I **know** that many (not all) of your clients want more help then you currently give them. I have asked them directly what they want – and so have many others.

There have been 2 significant and personal surveys done to prove that your clients want more.

1. I personally interviewed 1,077 business clients on behalf of 129 accounting firms in a 'Client Advisory Board' format. There were around 8 business clients at a time in a meeting room and I asked them what they wanted from their accounting firm. They all said basically the same thing, "We want them (you) to be more proactive with us. We know they know more than we get. We want to them to tell us in advance what we need to do."

2. My business partner in my coaching business (www.nixonadvantage.com), Colin Dunn, surveyed 1,500 small to medium businesses over the web. The main question was what else do you want from your accountant that you are not getting now? The primary answers. Cash flow, profit and management accounting help.

The evidence stacks up. Clients want more help. Are you in a position to offer it? If you do not offer it then someone else will – and you may lose the client.

Mostly you do not react until the client calls you (sometimes late on a Friday afternoon) and says, "HELP, the bank has just called, we have hit our overdraft limit, they are going to start bouncing cheques and credit cards. They want us to have a budget, cash flow and re-finance plan by Tuesday – HELP, HELP, HELP!" You say (or think), "Why didn't you call me sooner?"

Did the client know they were trading insolvent? Did they know they had a cash flow issue? To many businesses they think cash flow management is Internet banking.

If you are the expert in finance, cash flow management and structuring then why didn't you build string relationships, keep in touch with them and inform them of the pending issue?

All good in theory you say. The biggest objection I get is that you think there is no money to pay for these much needed additional services. Let me tell you - **there is always money available**. The client is paying the rent / mortgage / school fees / car lease / salaries / overheads. It's not a case of not having any money – it's the prioritisation of the money.

At the time of writing (I switched accounting firms 3 ½ years ago), I was your typical $4k - $5K per year compliance client. With the new firm (one of our coachingclub members) I have so far paid them $249,600 (plus GST) and I am deliriously happy. By the way, you do not want me as a client – I know too much about what goes on!

As I finish this chapter on what's wrong and right with the current model I am intrigued by the word 'Practice'. You call it an Accounting Practice. Are you a practitioner practicing your craft, constantly practicing before getting it right?

I think it's time to stop 'practicing', you should be good at it by now. You've got a business to run! Let's change the model and get a vastly different result.

2

Change is On the Horizon

If you are dissatisfied with the performance (personal satisfaction and/or monetary rewards) of your current firm then you will need to change what you are doing. Not tweak it a few percentage points in productivity, average hourly rate, write-offs or lock up. No!

You will need to change what you are doing dramatically if you want a different result. The good news is that the change needed is not that hard to do once you get your motivation and mindset right. This chapter will explore the key areas that need to change from a 'business model' point of view.

The New Equation

If the old equation is internally focused then the new model is externally focused. It is based on marketing, sales, building relationships, value pricing and customer service. This equation below is a mathematical equation which, when you know and adjust the numbers, becomes a very powerful formula.

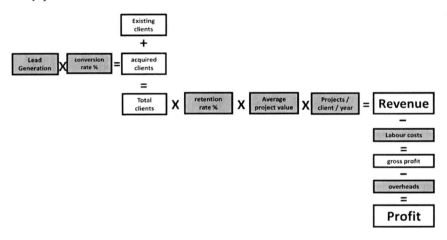

Knowing Your New Numbers

Just like you know your numbers in the old equation you must know your numbers in your new equation. What you can measure you can manage.

- ✓ You need to know how many (exactly) existing clients you currently have.
- ✓ You need to know how many (exactly) leads you get from each marketing campaign.
- ✓ You need to know your conversion rate (exactly) from enquiry to sale.

- ✓ You need to know your retention rate (exactly) of existing clients.
- ✓ You need to know the average sale value (exactly) of each project.
- ✓ You need to know how many projects (exactly) your clients buy from you each year.

What business can exist without knowing the numbers? Work out what your numbers are, and then you can apply a strategy to improve each one of them. After your analysis your numbers might look something like this:

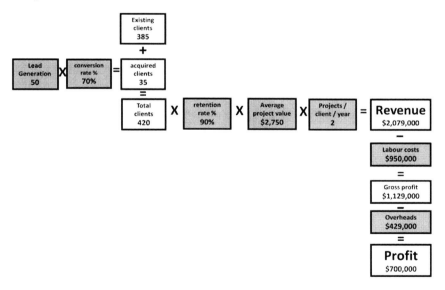

Your Brand

Before we break the equation down into bite size bits you need to determine what makes you unique and different. Are you in the 'sea of sameness' like every other accounting firm or are you different? What is your unique position in your market place? Do you want to be different? Do you want to stand out?

Once you answer these questions (hopefully positively in so far as you want to be unique) you can get on and position your firm in any way you choose. As my team and I coach, visit and observe firms we notice that their 'brand' is often tired and to put it bluntly boring. The firm's website (if they have one) was created some years ago and the partners photographs do not represent what they look like now. Your new client might not say it but they may think it …. *"Hmmm, you seem to have less hair now and you look like you are larger around your middle than you are on your website."* The colours are often bland and there is no modern style to anything. I went into a firm one day and they showed me their letterhead. I asked: "Why is it in black and white?" Answer, *"So we can print right out of the printer – it saves on printing costs."* You can't make this up. Your brand is every aspect of your firm – from the way you dress, to your building, to your colours, your collateral, your work, your style and even your furniture.

Tired, traditional, cheap and boring – that's what most firms' 'brand' looks like.

It's time for a brand makeover. Employ a branding consultant to do a complete overhaul of the entire 'look & feel' of the firm.

This is all called 'positioning'. How you are positioned in the market place before or whilst I do business with you. Here is a checklist of positioning tactics (many cost zero money) that you can apply so you are positioned differently to what you are now.

- ✓ High prices.
- ✓ Articles.
- ✓ Media releases.
- ✓ E-newsletters.
- ✓ Website, Blog, Social Media.
- ✓ Testimonials & case studies.

- ✓ Free reports, tools, videos & audio.
- ✓ Speeches – paid & free.
- ✓ Other peoples' newsletters.
- ✓ Reference list of existing clients.
- ✓ Competitions & awards ceremonies.
- ✓ Being controversial.

There are many ways to be positioned differently. Implement something.

Lead Generation

Most accounting practices have a 'zero based' lead generation (or new enquiries) strategy. Which means they do nothing. New clients just 'appear', typically via referral. Nothing wrong with getting referrals from existing clients. In fact they are the best quality leads you can get - free and credible. The challenge with referrals is that it is typically reactive and you have no control of how many you will get and when. So just having a 'referral only' strategy is a path to slow growth. To be proactive in lead generation you need multiple methods to attract the clients you want to attract. It starts with a database of your target market (niche, geographic, service focus) and then with proactive and persistent marketing (with the focus on generating leads) you attract potential clients to your firm.

Here are some examples of proactive marketing tactics that you can apply:
- ✓ Direct mail & email.
- ✓ E-newsletters.
- ✓ Paper newsletter / magazine.

- ✓ Seminars & Workshops.
- ✓ Boardroom briefings.
- ✓ Tele-seminars & Webinars.
- ✓ Referrals from clients or spheres of influence.
- ✓ Host beneficiary relationships.
- ✓ Advertising.

People buy from people and if you want to get my attention as a business owner (assuming that's your target market) then you have to remember one word – **experience**. Not your years of experience but the ways that I **experience** your smarts. You need to create multiple points of **experience** in your marketing campaigns. Mix it up with voice, video, meetings, presentation, words written, tools downloaded etc.

As you start your journey into proactive marketing you need to remember "**Rob's rule of 27**".

In technical marketing terms it takes 9 times of hearing or seeing the same thing before your target market 'gets it'. However, with the volume of marketing noise coming from all sources, your clients or prospects only get to see or hear around every 3rd one. Hence, the rule of 27. That means you need multiple lead generation methods because the first few campaigns may have gone unnoticed.

Conversion Rate

If lead generation is about getting people to come to you and make and enquiry then conversion rate is about converting that enquiry into business. Typically the conversion rate from quality referrals is relatively high. However, when you start proactive marketing (using additional lead generation methods) your conversion rate may drop.

You need to know what your current conversion rate is over a reasonable time frame (we call this the 'opportunity open days') and you need to acquire new skills and methods to increase your conversion rate.

Here is a list of skills, techniques & tactics you can apply to increase your conversion rate:

- ✓ Your conviction, self-belief & self-esteem.
- ✓ Finding your prospects / clients objectives and motivation.
- ✓ Follow up, follow up.
- ✓ Activity levels – no. of calls, no. of meetings.
- ✓ Nurturing during sales – points of experience.
- ✓ Time & scarcity-based offers.
- ✓ Sales aides-collateral.
- ✓ Scripts / dialogues / language.
- ✓ Needs analysis.
- ✓ Role-plays & practice.
- ✓ Presentation style.
- ✓ Educating prospects.
- ✓ Closing techniques.
- ✓ Consultative selling.
- ✓ 'What if' based selling.
- ✓ Testimonial & case studies.
- ✓ Objections and answer list.
- ✓ Asking for the business.

With new skills (in this sales area) you will reduce the days the opportunity is open, increase your conversion rate, increase your average project value, increase the number of projects each of your clients buy from you and you will also increase the margin (average hourly rate recovered) on each project as well.

Retention Rate

The retention rate of clients of existing clients is typically very high. As I will explain in more detail in later chapters, it is high because you have the clients 'bluffed' that it's hard to change accountants. By the time the client gets to leaving the firm you have completed most of this years' work. When you start pricing up front you will lose some clients. It's an out for them. That's a good thing because typically you will lose the types of clients you wanted to lose.

Increasing (or maintaining) retention rate is about building closer relationships with clients and increasing the customer service levels.

Following our theme, here is a checklist of tactics you can apply to improve retention rate:

- ✓ Client nurturing program.
- ✓ Outstanding client service.
- ✓ Call them and ask, 'how's it going?'
- ✓ Visit clients at their place of business.
- ✓ Invite them to social and business events / seminars.
- ✓ Send them cards, letters, emails and items of interest.
- ✓ Build a community of clients.
- ✓ Run client advisory boards.
- ✓ Refer business to them.
- ✓ Offer additional and new services.
- ✓ Send newsletters and updates.
- ✓ Ask the client how they want to be served.

Increasing loyalty and relationships is about being proactive and communicating more.

Average Project Value

The average project value is not the average fee per client. The average project value is where you average all of your invoices over the year. If you have three invoices for the one project then that is one invoice only. You might call a project a 'job' or 'task' for the client. For example, annual compliance is one project. A budget / cash flow forecast is a project. A re-structure is a project. A company due diligence is a project. What is the average for you?

Once you know your average (and you do want to increase it) you can use some or all (or others) of the checklist below to increase the average project value.

- ✓ Realise your services are worth more.
- ✓ Find the courage to charge more.
- ✓ Increase all prices immediately.
- ✓ Offer additional services at the time of buying.
- ✓ Have a standard menu of services and price list.
- ✓ Price in advance not arrears.
- ✓ Articulate the value of each project eloquently.
- ✓ Get rid of low margin services and low margin clients.
- ✓ Improve your language and sales skills.
- ✓ Target more profitable clients & services.
- ✓ Use value based fees – not time X rate!

You are doing the project anyway so if you can get more 'margin' out of it then the new margin is free and clear profit.

Projects Per Year

As you work out the average project value you also work out how many projects your clients are buying each year. Or another way to think of it is how many **products** do they buy from you each year. I remember having lunch with the CEO of a major bank. We were talking about retention of customers for the bank. He said something that really resonated with me. He said:

"If we can get a customer to buy 4 products from us then we will keep the customer for a very long time. If they only buy 1 or 2 products then it is easier for them to leave."

Same for your business, if the client only buys one product from you (say, annual compliance) then they are not really 'wedded' to you. In Internet speak – the **stickiness** is just not there.

The vast majority of your clients have unmet needs and your job is to find out what they really need and offer it to them. When I shifted accounting firms I went from an average of 1.5 projects per year to 6 with the new firm.

There are many ways to do this – here is yet another checklist.

- ✓ Productise your existing services into a definitive list – with prices.
- ✓ Create new services – leverage off other firms.
- ✓ Lower the barriers to doing business – free phone calls, emails.
- ✓ Build relationships by having a communication schedule.
- ✓ Educate your team to find opportunities.
- ✓ Think a minimum of 4 products per client.
- ✓ Work out what they haven't got on your client/service matrix.

- ✓ Constantly market services through all channels.
- ✓ Have a service theme for the month / quarter.
- ✓ Have your 'intellectual property selling opportunities' radar on at all times.
- ✓ Find out what the clients really need – do not prejudge.
- ✓ Offer your services – they can only say no!

The simplest business model in the world is 'find the need and fill it'. I think it is your duty of care to offer every service you have to every client you have. Who knows, some might buy the additional service. I also think you should continually innovate and invent new products and services.

The number of projects a client buys from you is one of the easiest in the new growth equation. There is already a high level of client loyalty and trust and they have unmet needs. You just have to ask the right questions!

Rob's Rule of 38:43

If you were to work out your numbers using my equation and then focus on strategies to improve each key area (I just gave you 74 separate strategies in the checklists) then you would have a vastly different result. Consider the numbers in the graph on the previous equation.

420 clients X

90% retention rate X

$2,750 per project X

2 projects per client =

$2, 079,000 of revenue.

If we were to apply *'Rob's rule of 38:43'*, (5+3+10+20=38) then you would have a 43% increase in revenue. Let me explain…

✓ A 5% increase in clients.

✓ A 3% improvement in retention rate.

✓ A 10% increase in the price per project that you sell.

✓ A 20% increase in the number of projects per year per client (which means only 20% of clients buy 1 more service per year.

This equates to:

441 (clients) X

92.7% (retention rate) X

$3,025 (price per project) X

2.4 (projects per client per year) =

$2,967,938

A 43% increase in revenue.

Apply the same process 2 years in a row and you will **double the size of your current revenue**.

With a focus on value pricing (not pricing in arrears on time X rate) and being more efficient (reducing labour intensity) you will not need as many people as you think to deliver the new revenue. Even if you added $200,000 in additional salary expenses (if you follow our efficiency model you will not need too much in the way of labour) and you added $100,000 in additional overheads (by taking part in our coaching program we can guide you on how you do this), you will still be better off by a whopping 84% increase in profit. See below.

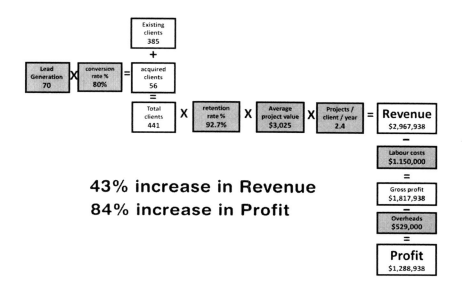

43% increase in Revenue
84% increase in Profit

Break the entire model down to bite size bits and it becomes more achievable.

It's All About the Clients

The old (traditional) growth model is all internally focused. Nowhere in it is the client mentioned. The new growth equation is all about the clients. It's about marketing to get additional clients from firms who are not giving legendary service (hopefully like you do). It's about serving them well to keep them delighted, loyal and referring more. It's about offering all services to them and it's about you receiving fair compensation for the value that you create for the client.

Yes, you need to be efficient and track job turnaround times and productivity. And you need to monitor the average hourly rate and other measures so you know if you are on track or not. These are all important things to quantify but they should not be the primary focus.

The primary focus should be on your clients. In our coachingclub meetings and within our client network we are constantly discussing 'sales visits' that each partner or client-facing team member is doing each month. We are asking (and keeping accountable) how many were completed, how many projects eventuated from the visits and what was the new revenue that was created as a result. Yes I want you to drive top line revenue and I also want you to drive customer service and loyalty.

If it's all about the clients then you need to be '*into the clients*'. You need to think creatively about how you can help them and you need to constantly meet with them and discuss ideas and opportunities with them.

Consider this model when it comes to clients and services.

Which is easier?

existing clients

2	1
4	3

new products & services (left) **existing products & services** (right)

new clients

The ranking system says that the easiest thing do is to have existing clients buy existing products and services. You have client loyalty and you have already done the project with another client so there is limited research and product creation to do.

The 2nd easiest thing to do is have existing clients buy brand new services that have just been created. Again you have brand loyalty and the conversion rate is extremely high so the cost of sale is dramatically reduced.

The 3rd easiest is to have a service you have done before with another client and you perform that service with a completely new client. You do not have to spend much effort creating the service and the new client will be quite receptive to it because they typically wanted additional services from the previous accountant.

And the 4th easiest (or hardest) thing to do is to win a new client and offer them something you have never done before. You better have a network of other firms to back you up and a suitable 'knowledge factory' to tap into so you can say 'yes' to everything.

So let's focus on the easiest thing to do (box 1) which is existing clients buying existing products services from you.

In my live seminars I have a 3 part quiz in relation to box 1. Remember, it's the easiest thing to do so I assume it has already been done!

1. How many of your existing clients have **purchased** every single product or service that you can currently deliver?

2. How many of your existing clients **know** that all these products and services exist? They could read the services list back to you verbatim. They may not need the services now but they could need them in the future or refer you to someone else who needs them.

3. How many of your existing team members (and this includes the partners) **know** about every product and service that exists within the firm's capabilities?

Okay, question 1 was a trick question. The answer will be close to zero because not every client needs every product or service that you have to deliver.

The real questions and opportunities are in question 2 and 3 because the answers to those questions will be similar to question 1 as well. Your clients need to know what all the services are and so do you and your team. Start right there.

If you focus on your clients and you make sure that the price you charge is based on the value you contribute then you cannot go wrong – unless of course you grossly under price the service or you take too long to complete each project.

History Makers

The old model suggests that most of the work that accountants do is history writing. Writing up the past and presenting it, is a timeframe that it is not relevant anymore. Clients want additional help and if you take the view that by being proactive and really helping your clients, you can become **a History Maker.**

Accountants have so much to offer if they just get proactive. After surveying thousands of clients of all types of industries I have narrowed it down to 5 key areas (over and above compliance services) where clients want help. We call it "The Fab 5".

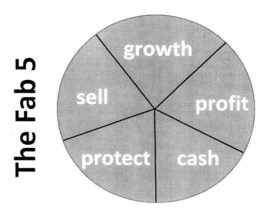

The Fab 5

If you just ask the right questions and listen carefully you'll hear your clients saying:

"Help me to grow my revenue and my wealth."
"Help me to improve my profitability."
"Help me to understand and free up my cash flow."
"Help me to protect my assets for future generations."
"Help me with succession planning or with the sale of my business."

Your skills and services (that clients have not bought yet) can do these things. If you do not possess the skills, tools, products or processes in your firm, then seek them out via our network –
go to www.proactiveaccountantsnetwork.com for more information.

Offering the Fab 5 services really does help your client to define their future, create wealth, build a better lifestyle and create a legacy.

By just offering history writing services which (although important and must be done) is a grudge purchase, you are not really helping your clients at all.

To get your firm into a position to offer additional value added services to clients and prospects I see there are 5 distinct steps to make it happen.

1. Get specialised coaching (by my coaching team of course) to guide you on how to do it – this is new territory and you should only follow those that have already done it with others.
2. Get better with what you have got – sort out workflow, WIP, debtors, write-offs, pricing, people, systems etc.
3. Free up capacity – hire more people or reduce labour intensity by being more efficient.
4. Develop your product / service offering – look at your range of services and productise them or seek external help to do so.
5. Market and sell your services – get active by marketing and selling to existing and prospective clients.

Start making history today. Call all of your clients and go visit them. Offer something new. Your clients will be better off for it and you'll be rewarded accordingly – unless you price your services the old way – time X rate.

Structuring for Success

The new equation means you need different skill sets. You will need a different structure to create, market, sell and deliver the new services to new and existing services. And you will definitely need different people involved.

The traditional 'partnership' model is one of a silo model. Often it has been described as 'accountants sharing rent'. The silo model is where each partner or division has:

☒ My marketing style & ability.
☒ My sales style & ability.

- ☒ My clients and client management.
- ☒ My team.
- ☒ My services.

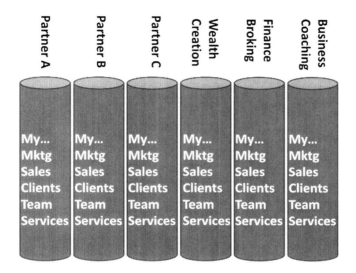

I have a cynical view as to why the silo model exists…so it can be pulled apart very quickly if the partnership doesn't work out.

The issue is that even if there is one logo and brand on the business card there are separate practices operating behind it. The separation means that unless the partner (or team member in the partners silo) can perform the project themselves they will not 'internally refer' to others. There are different services being delivered, multiple 'bosses', multiple and erratic marketing methods, different ways of doing the same type of work, different pricing mechanisms and overall inefficiencies everywhere.

Enter the new corporate model. One that has one CEO who is given the authority to run the business as he/she sees fit, to oversee the people who are creating products and services, the   marketing specialists, the sales people who sell and manage client relationships, the logistical management people who keep the office environment moving and working and of course the delivery people (fee delivering professionals) to do the work.

Your New Organisational Chart

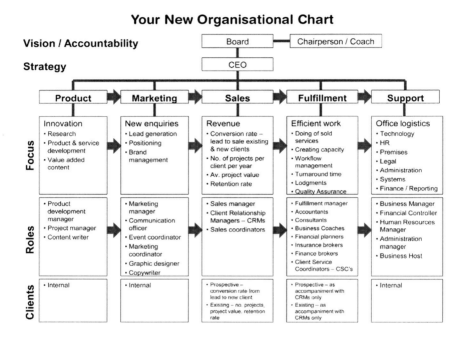

Each of the five key areas needs differing skill sets and disciplines.

> ➤ Product development people are typically very creative but with a disciplined and detailed approach to product quality and systemisation – you can call in help here with our Accountants Knowledge Factory.

> ➤ Marketing people are also often creative and the marketing coordination team members are often introverted with a detailed focus. Maybe you start with a marketing coordinator and then grow into the other roles.

> Sales people must first have an inclination for sales. The skills can be taught if the inclination is there. The partners and some client facing team members of firms make excellent sales people because they have the client experience and natural trust. They may be doing some client work as well – they may be full time revenue generation.

> Fulfillment people are most of the people you currently hire. Let's not confuse what these teams are doing – they are delivering on revenue that has already been sold. They are not creating new revenue. They may be creating new opportunities so someone can speak with the client. The challenge with the traditional model is that you have had the fulfillment people also being product development, marketing and sales people. It just does not work. Some people just want to be an accountant – and that's OK.

> Support team members need to be just that – support for the rest of the business. Many firms have internal accountants (who are still doing client work) be the practice manager or the financial controller. If you want to grow, you MUST employ a full time business manager (not a practice manager) who runs the day to day operations of the office – IT&T, debtors, accounts payable, human resources, office logistics etc.

Now before you think "we are not big enough to justify hiring all of these people" you need to realise that all the positions in the organisational chart need to be done by someone. There may be some 'multi-hat wearing' going on and that's OK as you grow into the structure. You may also need to outsource some of the roles until you can justify a full time (or part time) person to fulfill the position. Your goals, courage and resources will determine how quickly you can grow into the new structure.

3

The Entrepreneurial Accountant – An Oxymoron?

~**Entrepreneur: Definition:**
*"One who takes the initiative to create a product or establish a
business for profit. Generally, whoever undertakes on his/her own account
an enterprise in which others are employed and risks are taken."*

Are partners of accounting firms entrepreneurs? This is an interesting
question. According to the definition they own a business (although
most did not start the business they own), they employ people, they
take risks, and they provide products and services – hopefully for

a healthy profit. Does this make them entrepreneurs? Would most partners of accounting firms describe themselves as an entrepreneur? Probably not.

So what do they call themselves? Normally they say, "I am a partner in an accounting practice," or words to that effect. Rarely do they say, "I am an entrepreneur who owns an accounting business."In this chapter I will challenge every aspect of your partnership model and hopefully convince you to operate under a different – more commercial – model.

Why Are Partners, Partners?

Although most accounting firms are operated by sole practitioners (one owner), by my educated guess there are approximately 3 partners for every accounting firm in the world. And from my basic research there over 1,000,000 firms in the world. So, there are somewhere in the order of 3,000,000 partners. Worldwide it is estimated to be more than a one trillion dollar industry. That's more than the GDP of Australia!

That is a lot of accounting firms and a lot of owners of accounting firms. Far too many of both in my opinion!

So how do the partners become partners? Here are some typical (and perplexing) scenarios. As an accountant goes through the ranks and learns their craft, at some point in time they 'make partner' – as if it is their given right. Sometimes a team member puts pressure on the partners and threatens leaving if they do not become a partner – and the partners cave in. Sometimes current partners <u>think</u> they must elevate a team member to partner status just to keep them – so they do. I even know of partners who have become partners without knowing the financial situation of the firm they are buying into. Who would want to be in business with someone who did not understand the financial situation of the business they were buying into?

There are too many partners who are there for retention reasons – not good business reasons.

What about the partner who starts his/her own firm? These are the real entrepreneurs in this industry. It's interesting how they come to be. The individual in question starts life as a junior accountant or graduate, learns how to do that part of the job, stays in the current firm for a few years, gets more experience and then shifts firms. They stay at the next firm for a few years and then maybe shift firms again. All the way observing how each of the partners conduct business.

One day (usually in the persons 30's) they wake up and say to themselves, "I am sick of being an employee of an accounting firm. I'm a good accountant. I want to go out on my own. I want to start my own firm." They have just had an entrepreneurial seizure!

Off they (you?) go believing that just because they are a good accountant that they know how to run a successful accounting business that provides great accounting services. Nothing could be further from the truth. Being a technician (knowing how to do the work) and being a business owner (knowing how to run a business that works) are two vastly different scenarios.

Here's the issue. How did this new entrepreneur learn how to run the business they have just started?

From the partners that they worked for. They learned by osmosis. And where did those partners learn their great (tongue firmly planted in cheek) business skills from? The partners before them. And so on and so forth.

If you want to run a better business you must first become a better business person.

If you stick to the traditional model described in chapter 1, the only real way to create wealth in this business is to have fewer partners in your firm and a higher leverage of people per partner.

There are plenty of sole practitioners around the world who hire 20+ people and as such they are making $1M plus profit per annum. The issue of low profitability starts when you have too many partners and the leverage (people per partner) is low. It's very easy to prop up profits in an accounting firm – just have the partners charge more time. They have the highest (apparently) charge rates, so all time charged by partners is theoretically, all profit.

Recently I asked a simple question at one of my coachingclub meetings. "If you could wave a magic wand, then the ideal business partner is someone who……?" And then got them to answer the question. This is what the group came up with.

The 'ideal' partner in an accounting firm is someone who…

1. Brings something to the table - complements existing partners.
2. Is a good cultural fit in the firm.
3. Is a good communicator at the partner level.
4. Is a good communicator with team members.
5. Is a good communicator with clients.
6. Is stable - emotionally and financially.
7. Is profit and growth motivated.
8. Has a good work ethic.
9. Is reasonably fit and healthy.
10. Is at the same stage in life mentally.
11. Shares similar values and ethics.

12. Has an ability to respect other partners.

13. Knows what they want - goal orientated.

14. Is supportive of new ideas.

15. Is flexible in their thoughts and actions.

16. Is a good business builder.

17. Is fun to be with.

18. Shares the vision.

19. Walks the talk not just talks the talk.

20. Acts in the best interests of clients and the firm at all times.

21. Can bring in new business.

How many of these 21 can your current partners answer favourably? Maybe some partners that you have are not a fit. Do you need fewer, more or different partners?

Maybe some change needs to happen in your firm at the partner level.

Partner Remuneration

How much should a partner of a multi partner accounting firm be paid? Should it be equal pay because you have equal shareholding? If it is going to be equal pay then each person must pass the checklist of the ideal partner. It's my opinion that most should not be paid equal.

I have a view that a lot of partners in this industry are overpaid senior accountants. They are doing the work of a senior accountant but getting paid substantially more.

As I mentioned there are many partners who are partners because of retention reasons rather than good business reasons. In today's money you can employ a senior accountant for $150K (or thereabouts) to do the work of most partners.

If I am paying someone $300K - $500K (with dividend) then I would expect them to operate differently to a senior accountant, who does the 'delivery' side of the work. As a minimum I would be expecting partners to bring in new business from existing and future clients.

High contribution partners should be doing just 3 things:

1. High-end work for a low percentage of time – advisory work at 'value based fees' high margins.
2. Nurturing existing clients – increasing the average fee per client with additional services sold – priced on value not time.
3. Leadership – driving performance of the firm and making sales to new clients.

So how much should you pay them?

To start the discussion you need to separate employee vs. owner. There is no right or wrong answer (to how much) however I think a rule of thumb needs to be, "What would it cost me to replace this person with another employee?"

By nature of the answer it means that there needs to be differing salary levels among partners.

I am talking about rewarding people with a package based on their contribution to the business. It is farcical to think that all employees of a business (partner group) should be paid the same amount if they are contributing in different ways.

As an example, if one partner is bringing in $300K worth of new clients per year and doing $200K of personal chargeable work, then they are far more valuable than someone doing $500K of personal chargeable work and not bringing in any new business.

To get it close to right (and the number will never be right) there are 3 considerations to the total salary package of an employee / partner.

1. **Salary** earnings - an amount that it would cost to replace you as an employee.

2. **Bonus** earnings - an amount based on 'above salary' contribution – it must promote over achievement.

3. **Equity** earnings - an amount based on your equity percentage and your dividend policy.

Excluding equity, as an overall employee package, you should be thinking about "on target earnings" - OTE.

Here are some examples of differing pay scales based on differing contribution.

NB. Before I get crucified the salary levels here are a guideline only. You'll need to check the various salary surveys to get accurate numbers for your location, type of work performed and the various skill levels of people.

Partner # 1. If you have a partner who wants to be the Business Manager of the firm, have zero clients then they should be paid accordingly. Maybe their OTE is $100K - $150K.

Partner # 2. If you have a partner who wants to be a workflow, delivery person (say 65% productive or $350K personal chargeable time) and manage $1M of team revenue, and do zero client nurturing, then they should be rewarded accordingly - like a Senior Accountant. Maybe their OTE is $125K - $200K.

Partner # 3. If you have a partner who does 50% chargeable time (say $300k of personal revenue), and manages $1M of team revenue and allocates 10% of their time to client nurturing (and they actually do it) then that would be approx. 100 sales meetings @ an average of 50% conversion @ an average $5K extra work for each sale - or an additional $250K of work that has been brought into the firm. Maybe their OTE is $150K - $250K.

Partner # 4. If you have a partner who does 30% chargeable time (say $200k of personal revenue), and manages $1M of team revenue and allocates 30% of their time to nurturing existing clients then that would be approx. 300 client sales meetings @ 50% @ $5K = $750K of new business. Maybe their OTE is $200K - $300K.

Partner # 5. If you have a partner who does 20% chargeable time ($150K of personal revenue), manages $500K of team revenue and who allocates 50% of their time to nurturing existing clients (approx. 500 sales meetings @ 50% @ $5K = $1.25M of new business. Maybe their OTE is $250K - $350K.

Partner # 6. The most valuable partner in the firm is the one that has zero chargeable time and they spend say 20% of their time with potential new clients (say 100 leads generated by the marketing team) and say 50% of their time nurturing existing clients, then the numbers are vastly different. 100 prospect meetings x 75% conversion x $10K each = $750K (recurring) business + 500 meetings @ 50% @ $5K = $1.25M of new business from existing clients. Total new revenue of $2M. Maybe their OTE is $300K - $500K.

This is part art and part science. Which partner are you? Which partners are your partners?

Are your partners best at the 'delivery' role or the 'developer' role?

This is going to hurt, but delivery people are a dime a dozen.

People who can generate revenue from existing clients or convert a prospective client with full services are not.

The Last Trusted Advisor

I believe accountants are the last natural trusted advisor.

Think about it…

> ➤ In the 1970's the insurance people lost their position of trust when they started selling 'whole of life' policies and other 'products – trusted advisor status revoked.

> ➤ In the 1980's the banks started closing the branches down and subsequently the bank managers had their status revoked.

> ➤ In the 1990's we had the rise of the investment banker and by 2010 they destroyed their position of trust with the global financial crisis.

> ➤ The financial planners started off OK but got their trusted advisor status well and truly revoked with 'less than above board' commissions and failed investment (typically property or agricultural related) scheme after failed investment scheme.

And the lawyers….some would say they never had trusted advisor status in the first place!

Sure there are some less than scrupulous accountants who put their fingers into the trust accounts (always with the view of paying it back) or blatantly stealing from clients.

I remember one memorable meeting at a 'soon to go into liquidation' accounting firm for well below the line (illegal) activities. I casually asked one of the long-standing employees, "So how much

of clients' money did you put into these failed investment schemes?"
Answer, "I dunno, somewhere in the order of $200M - $300M over
a ten year period."I was utterly gob smacked. Even though the track
record was failure over the years, they still had enough trust to extract
$20M - $30M per year from the client base. The firm was getting
10% - 15% commission on the money regardless of the success of the
program. Incentives like that drive the absolute wrong behaviour. No
wonder most of the financial planners who have been selling 'commission based products' get themselves into so much trouble!

Even with big accounting scandals like Enron and Arthur Anderson
the trusted advisor status of the accounting profession remains.

It's almost like when you become qualified you get your fancy
certificate that you proudly hang on the wall and it comes with a
permanent tattoo for your forehead which says, **"Trust me– I'm an
accountant."**So why do we trust accountants? Is it the ethical standards that they are bound by? Is it that there have not been that many
(in the scheme of things) scandals? Is it that we are told to trust them?
Is it that the professional bodies (that all real accountants are members
of) actually mean something? Is it the piece of paper on the wall? Is
it that clients are typically referred to an accountant and we trust the
referee?

All of these certainly help, however I think the main reason we
trust accountants is because they know more about our financial affairs
than anyone else. And financial affairs are a very personal and confi-
dential matter. Accountants know the intimate details of our profit,
debt, wealth, revenue and cash flow.

Accountants can influence positively (by offering additional help)
and negatively (by doing nothing), influence our profit, debt, wealth,
revenue and cash flow.

To give you an idea of the size of your level of trust, consider the following equations.

Profit TRUST Equation. Again with the annual compliance results add up all the profit that your business clients achieved over the past 12 months. If your average client did $250K in profit and you had 200 of them then that would be $50M of profit that you could positively or negatively influence.

Revenue TRUST Equation. Using the annual compliance results add all the revenue that your business clients achieved for the past 12 months. You might have 200 business clients and they had average revenue of $1M each then that would equate to $200M of revenue that you could positively or negatively influence.

Debt TRUST Equation. With this equation add up all of the business and personal debt of all of your clients – business and personal clients. You might have 200 business clients with an average business debt of $350K and 300 personal clients with an average household debt of $250K so that would be $190M of debt that you could positively or negatively influence.

Cash TRUST Equation. If your business clients have an average free cash flow balance of $100k per year and you had 200 clients then that would be $20M of free cash flow that you could positively or negatively influence.

Wealth TRUST Equation. Take the net balance sheet position of your business and personal clients. If you had 200 business clients with a net balance sheet average of $1M and 300 personal clients with a balance sheet position of $500K then that would be a whopping wealth under your custodianship of $350M that you could positively or negatively influence.

Having trusted advisor status is a very privileged position to be in. It's a big responsibility as well.

I think it is the accountants 'duty of care' to leverage off the trusted advisor status and positively help clients by offering additional services that really make a difference to the clients financial condition.

It's How You Think

If you want to run a thriving accounting business you need to need to change the way you think.

How you think and what you think about is crucial to your success. I meet many accountants who have low self-esteem.

It's my belief that the 'order taker' and 'clock watcher' mentality drives a level of thinking that is not conducive to business success. Self-esteem plummets when you don't have to work that hard for new business (the government changes the rules and you get some more), when 90% of the revenue comes in every year regardless of what you do and when you are not required to market, sell or build client relationships – they still keep coming back!

With low self-esteem, accountants tend to talk a lot *at* clients – telling all the time rather than asking and listening. It's like you have been taught to bamboozle clients at accounting school with fancy terms so that you look good in front of the client.

Low self-esteem also drives accountants into the most arrogant activity of all – prejudging what clients will or will not do. I have heard partners say, "Don't send them the newsletter – they'll never read it." And, "They will never turn up to the seminar." Or, "They will never buy that service."

How dare you prejudge a clients' future!

I also hear, "We can't find any good people." Are you sure? There are thousands out there, they just don't work for you! Or this one, "We don't have any clients that will buy that." How do you know that you don't have the right clients? Have you asked them all? And when a good idea is presented that has worked in countless other firms before you, I get this one, "We could never do that." Hmmm.

This level of stinking thinking is driving down business performance and eroding self-esteem.

You have to change your attitude and mindset to one of abundance, confidence, self belief that you can do it, belief that you are worth more and belief that if you get out of your comfort zone, learn from others and be proactive you will get different results. Once you change your thinking you will start to run a better business.

Here are 2 great quotes that I live by and teach my clients to live by as well.

"Whatever the mind of man
can conceive and believe he can achieve."
Napoleon Hill, author of the bestselling book
"Think & Grow Rich" 1937

AND

"If you think you can you can.
If you think you can't you can't.
Either way you're right."
Author unknown

In June 2010 my wife, Natalie, and I had the privilege of spending 4 days with my favourite entrepreneur and business hero, founder of the hugely successful Virgin group – Sir Richard Branson. The reason I got to spend time with Sir Richard at his private retreat in Morocco was because the previous year, for my 40th birthday, Natalie bought me a ticket into space on Virgin Galactic. There were 12 'future astronauts' (as I shall be called from now on) and their respective partners at the gathering and we all had a blast (pardon the pun) trekking, cycling, eating, partying and generally hanging out together. After reading about his entrepreneurial and adventure exploits for years I was very excited to spend some quality time with Richard. So much so I compiled a list of questions to ask him! I wanted to know how he worked and how he thought. On the first morning I changed my mind and decided to toss the questions in the trash can. It felt too contrived. Once I relaxed and got into the groove I was quite surprised to learn how he ticked. Over breakfast one morning I even witnessed a fellow entrepreneur 'pitch' his idea to Richard. After 4 days, my synopsis as to what makes this man any different to all us mere mortal entrepreneurs is fivefold.

1. *He thinks much BIGGER than anyone I have ever met.*
2. *He has bucket loads of courage and self belief.*
3. *He surrounds himself with the best people – and let's them get on with it.*
4. *He chooses high volume business vehicles.*
5. *He always takes calculated risks and as he frequently says he 'protects the downside.'*

How big is your thinking? Are you limited by negative self talk and limiting beliefs? Is your potential stymied, by the people you associate with and the information you are putting into your mind?

When I ask accountants to change one of the most basic of business tactics – price up front versus price in arrears – I am typically met with fear and trepidation. What will the clients think and how will they react are the typical thoughts. When they finally implement the change it is never as scary as they thought and the client acceptance rate is close to 100%.

You can re-program your thinking and your self-belief system. You must first want to. There are thousands upon thousands of books, articles, stories, learning programs, seminars and courses that you can attend and absorb. Become a student of business and personal development. I was fortunate that at the tender age of seventeen I 'got into' self-help material and over the years I have amassed an impressive library of knowledge in many formats.

Remember this. You will become the person you want to be by the people you associate with and the material you absorb. Someone in the world has done what you want to do – seek them out and learn from them.

Let me leave you with a little saying that I heard recently:

> "Watch your **thoughts**, they become your words
> Watch your **words**, they become your actions
> Watch your **actions**, they become your habits
> Watch your **habits**, they become your **destiny**."

4

Your Clients On Your Terms

It's interesting how accounting practices evolve with their clients. It seems that over the years, the clients have just 'turned up' (via referral mainly) and you have accepted all that walk through your door. Almost like your firm is a community service or a charity. As time passes, the clients stay with you and many of them are not that enjoyable to deal with. Many of your current clients do not fit your direction and they supply information in a format and timeframe that suits them. It's not your clients' business it's your business!

It's time to take control of your clients and re-design the sort of clients you want to work with. This chapter will explore how you can change the working relationship with your clients – for the better.

Taking Control

Why is it that accountants work in progress (WIP) management is well above 10 days and debtors are more than 10 days? There is only one to blame – you.

Typically the client controls the cash flow of the firm. It has everything to do with the way the firm sets the client up and then works with the client. Remember, it's your business not your clients' business. The relationship needs to be on your terms.

Consider this. A client is accepted into the firm by referral (normally because they are unhappy with the current accountant) and the new accountant sends a once off engagement letter (in most cases only because they have to, according to professional body rulings) explaining charge rates (not a fixed price for the project) and broadly how the firm works with the new client. The client may or may not sign this letter.

When it comes time to do the work the accountant may send out a simple letter or checklist (most cases they do not) and generally the accountant simply *'lets'* the client send in the work in a format that the client chooses in a timeframe that the client chooses. The new work (called *work in progress* – WIP) arrives and an accountant picks up the work to get started. As the accountant gets into the job, they realise that something is missing. So they put the job down, communicate with the client about the missing information and then wait. A few weeks (sometimes months) pass and the missing information turns up. The accountant then picks the job back up again, reacquaints themselves with it and starts doing some more work and then realises something else is missing. Damn it! They put the job back down, communicate again with the client, and then wait some more. Finally the other missing pieces turn up and the job is completed.

Whilst all this madness is going on an accountant can be working on 15 – 30 jobs at a time – called 'open jobs'.

I was once in an accountants office (4 partners and 20 accountants) and casually asked, 'How many open jobs do you have at the moment?' 'No idea,' was the response. With a few key strokes of their computer they worked out that they had 440 open jobs! That's a whopping 22 open jobs per accountant. 'Let's take a look,' I requested. So we went past the facade of reception and into the engine room. You could see the open jobs. There was stuff all over the place. They said, 'Wait there's more.' One of the partners opened a cupboard door and there was more of it piled high on shelves. At that moment it started to fall out onto the floor. What a mess! A couple of days later I was at a dinner party and I met a dentist. I was telling the dentist about the firm I had just visited and the amount of open jobs they had at any one time. He said, 'That would be like me having 5 patients on 5 different chairs at the same time – no wonder they're inefficient.'

You can't make this stuff up.

The most efficient firms (in turnaround time per job) are limiting each accountant to work on no more than 3 jobs at a time and focusing on less than 10 days average workflow turnaround time for all jobs in the shop. I met a partner of a firm the other day and he has his accountants work on only 1 job at a time – turnaround time is less than 3 days average for all jobs. Now that's customer service!

As well as having too many open jobs per accountant I also find that fully trained accountants are doing a lot of 'administration work associated with the job' – sometimes up to 3 hours per accountant per day. An example of administration work (that needs to be done – just not by an accountant) is setting up work papers, collecting information from clients, chasing missing information, data entry, making appointments, monitoring and managing workflow, filing, lodging work, and generally advising clients of mundane information – like their tax file number!

In our coaching process we have a list of 30 standard administration tasks (associated with accounting work) with on average 22 of them being done on a regular basis by accountants. When we do 'time and motion' studies in firms we find that on average each accountant spends 1.5 hours per day doing (our definition of) administration tasks – sometimes up to 3 hours per person per day. If a working year is 225 days then that is 337 hours per accountant per year doing things that they should not be doing. If you have 10 accountants, that's 3,337 hours per year at an average hourly rate (let's say) of $200. That's a huge $674,000 per year in opportunity cost. A small firm of 10 accountants might only have revenue of $2.5M and to have 27% opportunity cost is just incredible.

What An Opportunity!

You can unleash this opportunity cost by employing specialised administration people – what I like to call 'Client Service Coordinators' (CSCs). If your accountants are spending 1.5 hours on average doing these administration tasks then you will need 1 CSC per 5 accountants. Their job is to keep the accountants busy by freeing them from all of the administration tasks associated with the accounting job.

If you think of your accounting business like a manufacturing business then you will manage your workflow management process vastly differently to the way you do now – and become more efficient in the process.

In a manufacturing business the Salesperson (Partner or Client Manager) scopes and sells the product, they then give the order to the Manufacturing Manager (CSC) who manages the overall production. The Manufacturing Manager (CSC) works out what raw materials are needed, has those gathered by the warehouse person (CSC) and sets the job up on the manufacturing line. The manufacturing team (Accountants) produces the product and then it goes to the quality control manager (Client Manager) for final sign off. The Shipping Manager (CSC) sends the product to the client and the Salesperson (Partner or Client Manager) follows up to add some value and then sell the next product.

To make that all make sense in an accounting business here is a 16 step workflow process that when implemented drives faster turn-around time, less time on the job, exceptional cash flow and high client satisfaction.

16 step workflow process

Steps in process	Who manages or does
1. Meet with client to scope and sell the value of the job	**Partner or Client Manager**
2. Value price the job, communicate in writing (scope & price) to client	**Partner or Client Manager**
3. Client signs off on scope / price and pays deposit or full amount	**Client Service Coordinator (CSC)**
4. Send checklist and gather raw materials	**Client Service Coordinator**
5. Check everything has been received	**Client Service Coordinator**
6. Contact the client for any missing information	**Client Service Coordinator**
7. Log the job onto your electronic and visual workflow system	**Client Service Coordinator**
8. Do a draft internal team budget – in hours	**Client Service Coordinator**
9. Set up the electronic workpapers – basic data entry	**Client Service Coordinator**
10. Challenge the hours budget (drive time down), lock in max time	**Client Manager & CSC**
11. Allocate & explain the job to the person doing the work	**Client Manager**
12. Do the job & find any FAB 5 opportunities for the client	**Accountant**
13. Communicate any technical queries to client & then finish job	**Client Manager and Accountant**
14. Review the job and fully understand FAB 5 opportunities	**Client Manager and Accountant**
15. Print / Collate / Bind / Prepare final Invoice / File	**Client Service Coordinator**
16. Meet client – present job, explain new ideas and sell next job	**Partner or Client Manager**

Our coachingclub and Proactive Accountants Network member firms have access to the position descriptions, tools, systems and processes to make all of this happen quickly, efficiently and seamlessly.

A sole practitioner (Brian) with $500K in fees joined my coachingclub program nearly 5 years ago and at that time his total 'lock up' (WIP and Debtors combined) was over 200 days. It was his first meeting and I told him he needed to reduce this dramatically in the next 90 days. By the time the next meeting rolled around he had reduced it to around 50 days – combined. Amazed at the result I asked how he did it and how much time he spent reducing it – I was hoping he had not written it all off! He told me he went line by line through his WIP ledger, billed everything he could and then put in place a diligent collection process. Total time of 40 hours work over a 3 month period. I then asked what the material benefit was to the firm. Brian answered with, 'I have $100,000 extra in the bank.' I responded with, "WOW, $100,000 for 40 hours work. At $2,500 per hour, a very good use of your time Brian."

Update on this story.

I just checked Brian's figures (now a 2 partner, $1.5M firm) on our online monitoring and benchmarking system and his lock up is typically 39 days – 14 days in WIP and 25 in Debtors. He cleaned it up once and kept it there.

Take control of your workflow and re-educate your clients on the way that you want to work with them. Change the system to suit your terms and be strong. It's your business not your clients'.

They Should All Be 'A' Class Clients

Every client you have should be an 'A' class client.

You have all sorts of clients. Some have great potential, they are open to new ideas, they pay your bills on time, are pleasant to your team and are generally great to deal with – they might be your A's. Others have no potential, they are closed minded, they moan and groan about everything and a general pain in the rear – they might be classed as a 'D' class clients.

There is no right or wrong criteria – each firm is different with the types of clients they want to deal with.

If I was running an accounting firm, here are my criteria for an ideal client.

1. Is an existing trading business with employees – not a start-up.
2. The business has potential.
3. The business makes an existing profit (pick a number!).
4. The business type is in line with my niche market(s) that I want to serve.
5. The owners are ambitious.
6. The owners are open to new ideas.
7. The owners are nice people to deal with.

8. They understand and play by my rules – pay me on time, adhere to my workflow requests etc.

9. I can make more than 80% gross profit (client fee less direct labour costs) on the client.

10. They are not 'price shoppers' looking for the cheapest accounting firm.

That would be my list – you make up your own criteria. Whatever your ideal list my guess is, only 20% (or less) of your current client base fit your new criteria. My guess is also that your current 20% represent around 80% of your fee base – or at least a substantial part. So the question is begging to be asked – **why do you keep the rest????**

Normally you keep the rest because of cash flow reasons. If you just had one criteria of profit per client (your profit that is) then you would be staggered by how unprofitable most of your clients are. Do this exercise. Put all of your clients into a spreadsheet with the following 4 columns:

Client Name	Annual Fee	Total Hours to Deliver Annual Fee	Average Hourly Rate

Divide the annual fee by the total hours (include non-charged time as well) and you can work out the 'average hourly rate per client'.

If you had a firm-wide average hourly rate (revenue divided by client hours charged – so if your revenue was $2M and you had 10,000 client hours charged then your firm-wide average hourly rate would be $200) of say $200 then you will find that your client range would be from around $120 to $300. Many of your clients would be well below your average – some of your largest clients (by fee) will be under the average.

Maybe you need to have a discussion that goes something like this with clients that you are undercharging.

"Mr & Mrs Smith we are thrilled that you have been a client of the firm for the past 10 years. You are great to deal with and we appreciate your business. What we have found, after some careful analysis, is that we have actually been undercharging you for the past 10 years – by about 30% per year. What we are <u>not</u> going to do is send you a whopping great big bill to rectify the problem. That's our mistake and your gain. Going forward however your work needs to be charged at X otherwise I am sorry we cannot do your work anymore."

Give your C & D class clients a shot at being A & B class clients. If you communicate your new direction and criteria they may want to play ball – at least give them a chance. If they do not want to be on the new team then get rid of them – quickly. They are sapping business oxygen from you and your team. They are making you miserable and they are sending you to the poorhouse.

Your decisions of the past got you to where you are today. So be it. You can always change. It does take some courage to change, however if you remember that you are only on this planet once (OK, some would say otherwise) and it is your business, then why not change. Why not take some courage pills and let them go. It is a very cathartic experience to ask a client to leave. The angst, energy and frustration caused by clients you do not want to deal with can be an enormous drain on team morale and sanity.

While I'm at it, most of your new business clients come from referrals. Make sure you never accept a referral from a D class client – their friends are idiots as well!

One of our coachingclub members started their journey years ago with hundreds of clients – all types of clients accepted by the firm over many years. They made a conscious decision to set a criterion for the type of work they wanted to do for clients – which was a minimum of quarterly reporting. They communicated with all of their clients to see which ones wanted the new level of service. Most did not, so they were referred to other accounting firms. They also educated their referral sources (bankers, brokers, layers etc) of their new direction and asked them to <u>only</u> refer prospects that fit their criteria. After a lot of culling they ended up with 109 clients and an average fee of $32k. Profit at this stage was running at around 40%. Eighteen months later after joining coachingclub) they did another 'cull' and now they have 70 clients with an average fee of $45K. Their profit now runs at around 50%.

Take charge. Make some decisions and design your client base with who you want to deal with in the manner you want to deal with them. I'll say it again – **it's your business not your clients' business.**

Clients Wants or Needs

Why do clients come to you from another firm? Ok, I know you are good and the best accountant around but really – why?

Do you ask every client why they left the other firm and chose you? Probably not. When it all boils down, clients leave one firm for another for just 2 reasons:

1. **Service** – lack thereof (not proactive, slow turnaround, poor relationship, poor communication etc.).
2. **Services** – they think they need additional services and sometimes they are not getting enough value for what they are paying.

The client comes to you with these requests. They want a better client service, with a few extra services at good value for money. So the client **wants** these things. Is that what they **need**?

I am suggesting that clients need more than they get from you. However, generally the client dictates the terms - what they want from you. You are the expert in what you do, so how would the client know what it is that they need?

To give clients what they need you have to find out what they need. If you find out what they need (over and above the mandatory compliance) then you will build a stronger relationship with them. If you build a stronger relationship, you will have more loyalty. If you have more loyalty you will get more referrals. More referrals come with choice of who you work with and a larger more profitable business.

If all you deliver to a client is the bare necessity of compliance then that is equivalent to a grudge purchase. A client does not want compliance – they have to buy it. It's a bit like buying petrol for your car. Compliance based services are part of the cost structure of doing business.

Remember this:

> *"If you are part of costs they can easily get rid of you.*
> *If you are part of profit then they can't get enough of you."*

What does that mean?

If you are focusing on what clients think they want (costs) then they can get rid of you. If you are really helping them to improve their condition (profit) then they can't get enough of you.

So how do you find out what clients need?

Simple – ask them! However, you are not about to say 'what do you need'? You see, this is the tricky bit - they do not know what they need. You have to be investigative and ask lots of leading questions before you determine what they need.

You can be investigative when you are doing other work for them. As you do the compliance work, think about the clients' situation and come up with some new ideas that you can take to them.

> *One of our coachingclub members (Craig) came up with a very simple but powerful idea. What he did was incorporate the 'Fab 5' into his end of job process. So as the accountants are finalising the work and filling in the checklist, the accountants have to fill in some extra questions like: How do you think this client can grow their revenue? How do you think this client can increase profit? How can this client improve cash flow? What does the client need to do protect their assets? How effective is the client's structure for succession planning? The accountants are trained to look for opportunities as they do the work and then it goes into the review process. The client manager then adds their ideas and then a meeting is called with the client to present the potential opportunities.*

Graphically Craig's process would look like this:

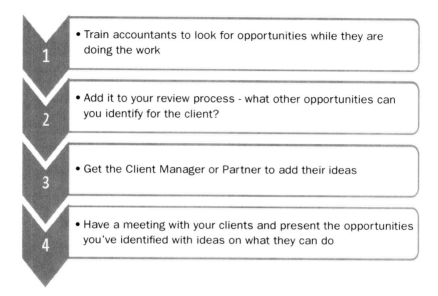

1 • Train accountants to look for opportunities while they are doing the work

2 • Add it to your review process - what other opportunities can you identify for the client?

3 • Get the Client Manager or Partner to add their ideas

4 • Have a meeting with your clients and present the opportunities you've identified with ideas on what they can do

Changing Accountants – Part 1

I was running a teleseminar with over 500 firms listening. I was interviewing an accountant (Shane) who specialised in medical businesses. He said that he dedicated every Wednesday to visiting his clients at no cost. The purpose of the meeting was to find out what the clients needed and if appropriate, to sell additional services to satisfy their needs. My existing accountant at the time (Peter) was listening in and he called me immediately after the meeting and said that it was a great idea to visit clients and he should start with me. I had been a client of Peters for 11 years and never once had he visited me – even though for 9 of those years my office was no more than 1 km from his office.

I guess it was too far to walk. I was paying Peter for compliance-based services only. That night I went home to my wife and said, 'You're not going to believe this, but Peter is coming to visit me next Tuesday – I think he is getting better!' So Peter turns up and I did what clients do. I explained my business, showed off my premises and indicated I had a few problems. I told him I had some overseas income coming in and didn't know what to do with it. I told him I wanted a referral to a lawyer as I felt I needed to do some IP protection and I questioned if my structure was right for tax effectiveness. Peter says, 'I'll get right onto it.' That was in the October and by April the following year I had had enough of waiting for Peter to get right onto it so I left and found a more proactive accountant.

Changing Accountants – Part 2

I know thousands of accountants and I finally chose a 3 partner firm whom I liked. I called the first meeting and told my new accountant (Matt the partner) that the first project they needed to work on was tax planning – I am a proactive client. Matt dismissed my request and said, 'Before we get into tax planning let me understand everything about the Nixon group – what you have now and what your objectives are.' – he was in control of the meeting at this point. Matt drew a line, two thirds of the way across on my white board. On the left hand side he wrote 'now' and started asking my wife and I a whole series of questions about our structures, profit, cash flow, kids, wills, assets,

liabilities, insurances and so on. He drew diagrams and pictures and when it all unfolded I turned to Nat and said, 'What a bloody mess that is.' Nothing seemed to link together or resemble any sort of order. Matt ignored my comment. He then went to the final third of the white board and drew a large 'T'. On the left he wrote Rob and on the right he wrote Nat. He then asked a whole series of questions around our goals and ambitions. He started with my wife then me. The whiteboard was eventually filled. He then said the following which I will always remember,
"You have great goals and ambitions and to achieve them you need to be financially well organised. You are not financially well organised, you are financially disorganised. Your structures are not right, you have debt in the wrong places, your wills are out of date, you do not have the right share structure and your trusts are not set up for maximum tax effectiveness. You are financially disorganised. With every new client (and every 3 years thereafter) we make sure you are financially well organised from the outset. We will work with you to get this right so your estates are looked after and you are set up for maximum tax effectiveness. Our fee to do this is $10K (I was thinking $15K) plus legal fees to get this right – when do you want to get started?"

I said yes, and that's how we started a great relationship.

If you ask the right questions in the right order you will find out what your clients really need – not what they want. Not doing so is doing your clients a complete disservice.

Building Enduring Relationships

When you get a lead for a new client you are so excited. It's almost like a potential new love has entered your life. To 'seal the deal' you really 'woo' the potential client in the dating period and you dance for a few weeks whilst you make all sorts of promises. Finally they commit to being engaged to you and the client agrees to your promises and charm. You are even more excited. The moment of truth is about to happen – marriage. The client signs your engagement letter and you send the mandatory 'ethical clearance letter' to the other accountant. Although you may not show it at the time, you may be having a party on the inside, your excitement levels hit an all time high. You are ecstatic – you have just signed a new $20,000+ per year client and you proudly tell your other partners of your lovemaking and courting prowess. They are equally impressed and they secretly wish they had your skills because they did not bring in any new clients this week.

And then it turns horribly wrong.

The client thought you would be doing the work (you didn't tell them otherwise), however they are handed onto another 'underling' who they have not met – sometimes the work is outsourced overseas without the client even knowing. The front office customer service, whilst dealing with the firm is less than cordial – you never met that person either. The initial work takes an inordinate amount of time to get done (again you didn't tell them otherwise), with constant 'back and forth' of information needed (why can't they do it in one go, your client wonders). Finally the 'draft' work arrives in the mail for signing and then a finished copy arrives some weeks later. During the course of the year the client calls you from time to time, however they hesitate to because every time they do, they get a bill. When the client comes to see you they do not spend much time on 'chit chat', they get right down to business because they know you charge by the hour. You told the client you would be 'proactive' in your advice yet all the client ever receives is a useless newsletter and letters from time to time when the government changes the compliance rules. You never randomly call the client to see how they are going and heaven forbid you never visit the client – you would have to charge for that!

You say you have good relationships with your clients yet how can you, when you deal with them in this way. How can you have a good relationship when you only see your clients once or twice per year? Imagine what sort of a relationship you would have at home if you saw your loved ones only once or twice per year. Some would say it would be better!

Building enduring client relationships is all about how you deal with your clients and how you communicate with them.

So how do you define a great client relationship? I think a definition of a great client relationship is when…

"Clients call you before they do things where you are the expert."

To get to that point you need 2 key things in place.

1. A consistent communication schedule.
2. Performance standards of how you work together.

An example of a consistent communication schedule would be.

1. An **Annual General Meeting** – to focus on the past year and plan the next year.
2. Quarterly **nurturing meetings** – to see how business is, add value and discover new opportunities.
3. **Phone calls** every 6 - 8 weeks – to touch base and see how business is.

4. Sporadic **'thinking of you'** emails / letters / phone calls - to show that you care.

5. Adding **more time** at the end of every 'presentation of work meeting' to have a one on one client advisory board meeting.

6. Invitation to your group-based **client advisory board** meetings.

7. Monthly **newsletter** – quality articles & case studies.

8. **Not charging** for quick emails and general phone calls.

9. **Social media updates** – blog, twitter etc.

10. Invitations to **seminars and events.**

The more communication you have with your clients the better the relationship you will have, the more they will buy from you and the more they will refer.

From the outset you need client service performance standards. Your performance standards will define the way you work with your clients. Once you have developed your performance standards (remember it is your business so you design them anyway you want) you should promote them at every opportunity. In particular as part of your client induction process each client should be stepped through each performance standard.

Here is an example of 12 critical performance standards which you can R&D – rip off and duplicate!

Performance standards

1. We lead the business community by example by running an exceptionally well run business
2. You will always know the price and scope of every project before we start
3. You will be totally delighted with what we do and how we do it – if you are not then there will be no charge for that project
4. You will be greeted and farewelled by name with eye contact and with a smile
5. If at fault, we will apologise and make restitution the same day
6. You will never receive a 'financial surprise' from the tax department or other financial institutions
7. We will proactively communicate to you for free whilst we follow our 10 step client communication process
8. Once all your information is received you will receive your completed project within 10 working days
9. You will always fully understand what we say because we do not use technical jargon when communicating with you
10. We will always tell you the 'candid truth' so you can make the right decisions
11. Any queries or complaints are owned by the team member who receives them and are addressed within the same business day that they are received
12. We always reply to all communication by the end of the same business day that it was received

It's a 'sea of sameness' out there when it comes to accounting firms. Each one looks and acts the same. If you want to differentiate, then it will not be via the quality of your work. Each firm says their work is of the highest quality yet how would the client know if it is or it is not when you have a disclaimer on everything – you don't even think the work is correct!

The only way that you can differentiate is by building an enduring relationship with the client whilst giving them outstanding service.

5

Put Your
Own Oxygen
Mask On First

No doubt you have been on an airplane and endured the mandatory safety briefing. Every safety briefing has the 'oxygen mask' discussion. On every flight I have ever been on they say (or infer) the same thing: *'Make sure you put your own oxygen mask on first before helping others.'* What they are saying is that if you are calm, relaxed and in control you can help others survive. The same applies to the accounting business. If you (as the advisor) are healthy, fit, relaxed, in control, successful and wealthy then you can help others to be the same.

In this chapter I am going to explore what it means to be wealthy and what you need to do to look after yourself – first!

Real Wealth

If you ask people about the definition of wealth most will say either: Lots of money, lots of free time, great health or enjoyable relationships.

Is it one of those or all of those?

Some people think being wealthy is just having a lot of money. Many people who have a lot of money do not have the free time to enjoy it and often they are overweight and unhealthy.

Others think that real wealth is having loads of free time. Unfortunately most people with a lot of free time do not have very much money – although they do have the time to be healthy and work on relationships.

Seeing this is an 'opinion based book' and it's my opinion, my definition of being wealthy is:

"To do what you want, when you want, with whom you want in a manner that you want."

To get to the bottom of my definition, let's break it down:

What's Your Ferrari?

To do what you want means you need to be living <u>your</u> dreams. Whatever they may be. You must first work out what you want from your life.

Ferrari – Part 1

I was in Naples, Florida at a worldwide consultants' conference and over dinner one night our host (Alan) told a story of how a friend of his always wanted to buy a Ferrari but never did. The friend was severely injured in a BBQ explosion and the friends' wife said to Alan, 'You know, he never did buy that Ferrari.' At that point in time another dinner guest (Mark) said to the table, 'So what's your Ferrari?' And around the table one at a time we were engrossed in stories of everyone's inner-most dreams and ambitions. It was an electrifying discussion. Fast forward to our annual coachingclub conference (Queenstown, NZ) and we had a very special 'presenter's dinner' with all of the speakers and accountants who were presenting on stage over the 4 day event. We were in a private room at an upmarket restaurant and Alan (being one of our guest speakers) was there. Alan told the story again, and again we went around the table asking each accountant (and other speakers) what their Ferrari was. It was amazing that deep down there were dreams not yet fulfilled and goals not yet met. One of the guest speakers (a business manager of a successful firm, Sean) leaned over to me and said, 'This is the best night of my life.'

Ferrari – Part 2

At our next coachingclub conference (Hawaii, USA) I decided to do something more elaborate with this Ferrari story. In my opening keynote address the room was dark and I appeared on the big screen driving a racing Ferrari in full racing suit. Once the film was over, smoke appeared and I came through the smoke in my racing suit and helmet. The conference room had a Ferrari theme to it and I told the Ferrari story complete with a slide show of potential 'dreams' that the audience may be interested in. I covered housing, travel, charity, sports, health, toys and overall lifestyle improvement. Once I was finished I gave the audience instructions to leave the conference room (this was only 15 minutes into a 4 day conference) with pad and pen and go and write down every conceivable dream, goal, aspiration and ambition they had and then come back in 1 hour. The audience (all accountants, remember) came back buzzing. We had some of the audience share with us what they had written down – applause and tears followed. Then each person wrote a detailed plan, on how to achieve their goals.

Each and every accountant in that room has a much higher propensity of achieving their dreams because they have committed to writing them down and coming up with a plan to achieve them. They are also held accountable to their plans through our coachingclub process.

So what is your Ferrari?

Spend some time working out what you want to achieve in your life. Write everything down. Let your mind run free. Be creative and remember all the things you wanted to achieve when you were younger. If you need some inspiration buy some magazines or lifestyle books. There is a plethora of books available on goal setting – go and absorb them and come up with a definitive list.

I am very goal orientated – diligently writing them down since I was 17. After years of goal setting I have worked out a number of personal systems that work for me. This system keeps me on track and focused on living the life I want to live.

- ✓ My life **mission** and **purpose** – this is a statement like a company mission statement.
- ✓ My **eulogy** – I have a written statement that I want people to say about me after I am gone.
- ✓ My **inspiration** – I look for inspiration through magazines, TV programs and dreaming.
- ✓ My **people** – I only associate with positive, goal orientated, forward thinking people.
- ✓ My **electronic** goals – I type my goal list into an electronic file.
- ✓ My **written** goals – I physically write every goal into my special 'dreams and ideas' book.
- ✓ My **dream board** – I have a cork-board where I stick pictures of what I want to achieve.
- ✓ My **focus** – I have broken my goals down to life, 3 years, 1 year and 90 days.
- ✓ My **accountability** – each month I meet with my master-mind buddies to keep me on track.
- ✓ My **achievement** – as I fulfill a goal I cross it off and put it on the 'achieved' list.

With all of my goals I follow the tried and tested S.M.A.R.T formula – with a twist.

Specific – the goal must be very specifically stated.

Measurable – the goal must be able to be measured somehow.

Audacious – the goal must stretch you and excite you.

Realistic – the goal must be realistic at the same time.

Timebound – the goal must have a completion date on it.

One of my favourite achievement models is:

Decisions + Actions = Results

The model says that if you want a different result, you need to make some different decisions and then follow through with the appropriate actions. Sounds simple enough. You set a result that you want to achieve, you decide what needs to happen or change and then you go about implementing the action.

Here is what typically happens – YOU DON'T IMPLEMENT!

Why is that? When all the planning took place, the painstaking process of decision-making and then you don't follow through. The 'action' part is definitely the tough part and most people do get distracted during the implementation process.

Here's my theory as to why the action bit doesn't happen. Action does not happen because the **result** you wanted to achieve was not **big** enough or **inspiring** enough to motivate you into action.

If you have bigger, more audacious goals you will be more motivated to implement them.

A correctly structured accounting business that is run well is a vehicle to achieve whatever result you want to achieve in your life. As one of our coachingclub members said to me one day, *'I know of a 4 partner firm in Asia where one of the partners is a billionaire through the accounting firm.'* You have the right business vehicle. The question is do you have the motivation. Do you have the dreams and goals to drive you forward?

You Can't Lavish Time Unless
You Have Time to Lavish

To do what you want when you want means you need to MAKE time available to do what you want to do.

There are many excuses that people make for not doing something. The poorest, weakest excuse that has no meaning is, '*I didn't have the time.*' How can anyone not have the time when we all have the identical same amount of time to use. We all have 24 hours in a day 168 hours in a week and 52 weeks in a year. No one gets one second more or one second less.

It's not how much time we have it's what we do with our time that counts. **It's never a time issue, it's a priority issue.**

So what do you do with your time? Does the day just go so fast and you wonder what you have done that day? Do you constantly get interrupted my emails, phone calls, clients, suppliers, team members? Do you get home tired, kick the dog (not literally), have a beer, watch some TV, go to bed and then wake up and do the same thing the next day? Do you feel unfulfilled and dissatisfied?

Or do you feel fulfilled every day because you were in charge of your time and you only did things that were uplifting, exciting and energising?

How do you get to the point where you only do what you want to do and you are super effective on a daily basis? Here are some ideas which have helped me and many accountants I have worked with, to become very effective with their time.

Your Top 3

Work out what you actually do by initially keeping a log of what you do on a daily basis. When the list starts to repeat itself, stop keeping the log. Go back through the list and work out the no.1 highest dollar productive activity that you do – the one that you enjoy the most that is the best use of your time. Highlight that one. Then work out the no. 2 highest dollar productive activity. Highlight that one. Find the no. 3 highest dollar productive activity and highlight that one. Get rid of the rest. Delegate them, don't do them, or create a system so they do not need to be done at all. Get focused on just 3 things that is the best use of your time on a daily basis. You will find that a lot of your list is administration focused. You may need to hire an assistant to help you – if you do not have a personal assistant then you are one. My top 3 are **marketing** (leveraged marketing activities that builds brand and generates leads – not one on one selling), **delivery** (speaking to many at a time and coaching many at a time) and **leadership** (driving performance in my business, keeping my team on track and looking for the next idea to propel my business forward). What are your top three?

> *Years ago I was relocating my family from Sydney to Brisbane.*
> *I asked the removalist if he owned a lawn mower. He did not.*
> *I said, 'Now you do,' and I gave him my lawn mower. I have*
> *never mown a lawn since.*

The moral to this story is that if you do not want to do the task then do not learn (or own) how to use the equipment to do the task. There are people more qualified, cheaper and faster than you to do most tasks.

Time Blocking

Think of your week as 14 half days. You can achieve a lot in half a day if you have <u>uninterrupted</u> time. If you block time out to do the important things in your life (e.g: working 'ON' time, sport, family, hobbies) and you are not interrupted then you have a good chance of achieving them. I block out kids sports & school events, writing time, annual holidays (10 weeks set a year in advance), exercise time, golf practice & play, date night and short breaks. I then deal with clients and other work matters around the blocked out time. I have taught many accountants how to use a strategy called '**lockdown**'. Lockdown is where you commit to (say) 2 hours of uninterrupted time, shut the door, put a sign up, notify the team and get on and do whatever you need to do.

The more time you spend working 'ON' your business will mean the less time you need to spend working 'IN' your business.

It's Your Diary

If you feel out of control with your day and you are constantly interrupted then it is no one's fault but your own. You have to remember it is your diary – not your clients, suppliers, team members or anyone else's diary. Because it is MY diary I take control and have some very strict rules regarding my diary and phone calls. I do not return phone calls in the typical way, which is where you engage in telephone tag. Telephone tag is where you call me, leave a message, I call you and leave a message and some point in time (usually an inconvenient time) we finally connect. No way do I do this – it's a complete waste of everyone's time. Instead, I have telephone appointments for <u>every</u> phone call. If you want to speak with me (and I'll speak with anyone) then book a 10 or 15 minute telephone appointment with me. I do the same thing if I want to speak with someone as well – I have some neat scripts around this. I typically have these calls booked on the 10, 15, 20 or 45 of the hour. Even if I want to speak with someone I will book the calls at this time. The reason for the odd time is because most meetings start or finish on the hour – and meetings (not mine) are always late. It is also a bit different. I ALWAYS make the call precisely at the allotted time – I do not let the other person call me – even if they have made the appointment. Why? It's my diary and I am in control of my diary.

I always remember signing up a new client (Damian) 1 year after I initially spoke with him. He said he joined because I called him precisely the time I said I would – 1 year after the call was initially booked!

Managing Email

I get as many emails as the next senior executive. I have a PA (Brenda) but she does not manage my emails – I manage every single one of them. To manage them, my golden rule is that on any single day I will not have a 'scroll bar' on my inbox. To have only a few emails at a time in my inbox I use some daily techniques that you might find useful. I do not deal with emails as they come in – I deal with them in chunks throughout the day. I might dedicate 30 minutes to replying to emails. When I reply, I reply quickly and succinctly. My email responses are short and succinct because my view on email is that it is a short messaging tool and file sharing tool – not a conversation tool. Come and see me or call me if you want to have a conversation. I file (if need be) quickly into a file folder for later. I delete junk and other useless emails very quickly. I turn the email into a task if I need to – to be actioned later. I never reply if I am 'cc'd' into an email. I rarely reply if there is not a question in the email. I do not have the email alert thing that tells you that you have a new email - what a distraction that is.

Before email there was the 'in' filing tray that housed the letters, papers, phone call reminders and other files. Imagine if you had an old-style filing tray that looked like your current email inbox?

Meeting Effectiveness

Meetings can be such a waste of time. Especially meetings that are unstructured and with an unfocussed agenda. I will meet with anyone as long as I know what the meeting is about. Here are some of my rules around meetings which will enable you to have fewer but more effective meetings. To get the agenda out of someone I have Brenda ask callers 'what would you like to meet with Rob about – can you put it in an email please.' The agenda comes through and then we determine how much time is needed to deal with the agenda – normally much less than the person initially thought. In many cases I will have a telephone meeting before a face to face meeting. I love 'stand up' meetings, 'walk and talk' meetings, 'breakfast' meetings and 'coffee' meetings. These meeting styles are shorter in nature because it is not as comfortable as a comfortable office chair with endless coffee. Although a keen golfer, I do not like 'golf' meetings. They are too long and besides you are there to play golf not talk business. When a team member comes into my office I always stand up (I do not want to have them get too comfortable) and we have a shorter conversation. At the start of every meeting (I learned this from my accountant, Matt) I always ask, 'What do you want to get out of today's meeting'? I write down the agenda. I always have time allotted to each meeting and at the start of the meeting we determine the time and I always finish before the allotted time – I will do a time check before the end of the meeting (say 15 minutes left) and we will wrap up next steps. I always finish meetings on time.

To get you focused on succinct meetings remember the following saying: *'Tell them what they need to know, not everything that you know.'*

Self-Imposed Deadlines

What is the most efficient week of your year? That's right the week before you go on a holiday. You are going to be offline for 3 weeks and the week leading up to it you are happening. You are very succinct in your communication (your email response might be simply 'no' instead of a long drawn out answer) and you are able to get things done much faster than normal. The reason you are so efficient is because you created a self imposed deadline. In the accounting business there are very few real deadlines that must be adhered to. Because there are very few deadlines you get quite sloppy with getting things done. Getting back to clients takes longer than need be. You get workflow blow outs and there is a mad rush at the end of every month. If you were to have a self-imposed deadline on every task then this would not be an issue. Instead of saying to a client, 'I'll get back to you,' tell them, 'I'll send you the engagement letter by close of business Tuesday.' Instead of saying to a team member, 'Come back to me when you have finished the job,' say to them, 'When will you be coming back to me?' You need to have some fun with this and trick your mind into changing gears – hyper gear! I create self-imposed deadlines for everything. I take my laptop to the café to do some writing and my deadline is the battery life. I use the airline seat belt sign (on and off) as my deadline for writing. I say to myself, 'I am going to get this finished in this time,' and then I reward myself somehow. Sometimes my reward is golf, a coffee, a swim, a walk or maybe even some shopping.

If it is a BIG deadline (like when I ran the London Marathon or my goal to be a 'scratch' golfer or even finishing this book) I will tell many others about my deadline. That way I am accountable to more than myself.

My friend Michael tells a wonderful story of when he was coaching a very large homebuilder. Their average time to build their houses was 120 days and they thought (because they were the second biggest builder in the land) that they were pretty good. Michael was in front of the executive team and he challenged them on their building timeframes. He said to them, 'How can you do it in 10?' They thought he was from another planet or on drugs. They protested about the exercise but Michael stayed firm. He asked them to brainstorm how they could hypothetically build their houses in 10 days. Michael said in a perfect and hypothetical world, 'What would you need to start doing, stop doing, continue doing, have a different process, run a different system, use different materials or any other changes to make it close to being built in 10 days?'

He broke them into small teams and off they went and brainstormed for 30 minutes. They came up with dozens of ideas, which were transferred to a series of flip chart paper. At the end of the exercise Michael simply said, 'Just go and do that,' – whilst pointing to the flip chart paper. And they did. They didn't hit 10 but they did hit 40 days. From 120 days to 40 days. A massive upgrade on cash flow, a massive upgrade on customer service, a massive upgrade on new referrals.

You can't make any more time. You can be more effective with your time. Work out what you have to stop doing, start doing and continue doing to **make the time you have count**.

Toxic Relationships

To do what you want, when you want, **with whom you want** then you need to get rid of toxic relationships and only associate with people you want to associate with. If the people around you are miserable, snarly, sarcastic, negative or just downright nasty – get rid of them.

Do not associate with these people. Only associate with people who are uplifting, who have similar ideal to you, who are challenging and energising at the same time. Find some new friends and don't associate with any relatives who are like this well.

You need to have the right people around you who will support you. You should not need to 'suffer fools' or have anyone around you who has an ulterior motive. Sometimes these people are on your payroll and they tend to act like terrorists where they recruit other terrorists. Eventually it's like a cancer spreading quickly through your organisation. Get rid of the lot of them. Make the hard decision and fire them or force them out – you'll be glad you did.

If you decide to go on a holiday with another family then make sure the family have similar 'spending ideals' to you. If you are generous with your money on holidays (you like dining out, drinking good wine and generally enjoy the finer things in life) and the other family is not generous (they prefer buying groceries and cooking at your villa, cask wine and are generally 'tight') then neither of you is in for a fun time. Both parties will be miserable and want the holiday to end. Message to self – never go anywhere with these people again!

If you go out for dinner and you decide to 'split the bill' be wary of your dinner friends who want a different (always lesser) amount because they only had the soup, the salad and one glass of wine versus your steak and 3 glasses of wine. Message to self – never go to dinner with these people again!

If you have a dinner party or BBQ at your home and the people you invite promise, 'We will have you over next time,' and they never do. Message to self – never invite them back to your home again for a function.

For as long as I can remember I have been running or participating in a 'mastermind' group. This is a group of like-minded business people who are doing different things from me. We meet each month (normally over a long breakfast), brainstorm ideas and we keep each other accountable.

Maybe you need to join a network of like-minded entrepreneurial accountants – where everyone is striving for the same thing as you. Our network of proactive accountants meets every 6 weeks in small groups where they learn new ideas, share wisdom and keep each other accountable with their coach.

Check out www.proactiveaccountantsnetwork.com for more information.

If you need help or support then someone in the world has more than likely done what you want to do. Seek them out and ask for their help. It's my experience that people who are truly successful give back and lend a hand to others.

It's your choice who you associate with. Make some decisions and take action.

Feeling Good About Yourself

To do what you want, when you want, with whom you want **in a manner that you want** then you'll start feeling good about yourself. If you do not feel good about yourself then you will probably hate your clients.

You need to be happy with what you see in the mirror. You need to be fulfilled and you need to be excited about life. You need to be happy with the way that you execute your goals.

It may mean you need to change some of your dietary and exercise habits to get into shape. The healthier you are, the more energy you have and the better you feel about yourself.

It may mean you need to upgrade your wardrobe to feel better about yourself. There is a lot of truth in the saying, 'the clothes maketh the man.' Do not be a cheapskate when it comes to the way you look. If you want to be a success starting looking like a success.

It may mean you need to upgrade your travel style. Substantially better accommodation does not cost that much more. Having a driver pick you does not cost much more than a taxi. Upgrading your airline ticket to Business or First class makes the world of difference to how you arrive. My wife and I always travel in Business or First (depending on what is available) and we put the kids down the back in economy. Much to their disgust, we tell them they have to earn better travel themselves – just like we had to.

It may mean you need to become an object of interest. To become an object of interest you need to be interesting to be around. You need interesting stories, worldly experiences, good social skills and be seen as someone who is achieving something.

Feeling good about yourself it about looking after yourself. It is more important than looking after your clients.

Marathon – Part 1

Two weeks after my 40th birthday (where I received a ticket into space on Virgin Galactic as my present), Nat casually said, 'By the way I have also signed you up to run in the London *marathon in Richard Branson's team'. A trip into space and now a marathon. I was wondering if she was trying to kill me. I had never run more than 2 km's so always up for a challenge I said yes without hesitation. The Virgin group was the primary sponsor of the 2010 London marathon so there was a detailed training plan that came out. Just to be safe I verified the Virgin training plan with a 4 times Marathon winner – he added some ideas and gave me some support along the way which was great. I had no idea what it meant to run a marathon so I set 3 goals. The first was to **finish without stopping**. The second was to **finish without walking** and the third was to complete it in **less than 4 hours 30 minutes** - the average was 4 hours 41 minutes. I told everyone I met my 3 goals – even all my clients and I announced it on my forum as well.*

Marathon – Part 2

To help me, and keep me accountable, I enlisted my personal trainer, Craig, to train with me – except on Sundays when I did the long runs on my own. After 6 weeks I was up to 8km in distance and I got a very bad knee injury. It turns out the knee injury (which actually occurred playing golf in New Zealand) was aggravated the week before whilst I was trekking up a mountain in the Caribbean. I was out of action for 7 weeks whilst I had 15 physiotherapy sessions. Time to restart my training program. I had a 26-week program with only 17 weeks to do it in. For the next 17 weeks I toiled away, meeting my trainer at 5am each week day morning for a one-hour session. I averaged 40km per week running the 17-week timeframe. I was training 6 days a week to get at least partially ready for this event. My last big run was 33 km (this is what the plan said) before I headed off to London to run 42.2 grueling kilometers. Natalie was trekking the Himalayas for a charity the week prior so we met in Singapore and travelled together to London.

Marathon – Part 3

The day of reckoning – race day. I was as ready as I would ever be. I was up bright and early to get the train to the starting line. It was about 90 minutes away. I was told to go to the green start which I found out was reserved for celebrities, potential record breakers and people wearing crazy costumes – even Sir Richard was dressed as a butterfly with 2 metre wings! I thought I was the celebrity, however I subsequently found out that I was in a celebrity team. There were 37,000 competitors and 750,000 spectators lining the streets to cheer me on. The atmosphere was brilliant and very motivating. There were 80 pubs along the way and each one had a theme and a party going on. There were people drinking, singing and partying whilst I was slogging it out step by step. Every few pubs the partygoers would thrust a beer out to you and shout 'do you want a beer'. I thought I would love a beer however if I had a beer then I would need to stop or walk and my goals would not be achieved. The halfway mark was the Tower Bridge over the Thames River. I was feeling good *and energetic and crossed the halfway marker in exactly 2 hours. Full of confidence I was thinking maybe 4 hours was realistic. I was pounding away as I listened to my 4 ½ hour motivational play list on my iPod when at the 30 km the battery went flat – right in the middle of Kenny Loggins' 'Footloose' song. I said to myself – the crowd will have to bring me home. More partygoers were thrusting beer at me and I started to dream about having a beer – you think crazy thoughts when you run a marathon. Natalie gave me 2 affirmations to help me when things got tough. She told me these affirmations got her through childbirth and helped her while trekking the Himalayas the week before. I said to myself 'there's only one way home Rob' and 'it's only 2 hours of your life Rob and then as the finish got closer, it's only 45 minutes of your life Rob'. These affirmations helped me enormously. The crowds got thicker as we neared the finish line and my pace got slower and slower. The last 5 km or so was just exhausting but the crowd, my determination and goals got me through. My name was on my shirt and the crowds were cheering for me. The end was in sight. I knew that once I could see Buckingham Palace there was one corner and a few hundred metres to go. Exhausted as I crossed the finish line (I was practicing my stylish photo finish for weeks but could not muster the strength to do it) I completed my marathon **without walking, without stopping** and in **4 hours 20 minutes and 57 seconds**. Woohoo – I achieved all 3 goals. I collapsed in a heap then got myself together and went and celebrated my greatness.*

Did I feel good about myself after running a marathon – you bet! It was a life achievement that I will remember for a long long time. I also learned some powerful lessons during the process. I call this '**Marathon Success**':

1. Set goals and tell others about them.
2. Someone else has done what you want to do, follow the leaders.
3. If you want something bad enough, often you have to sacrifice.
4. Create a plan and stick to it.
5. Avoid temptations that may derail you.
6. If the dream is big enough the facts don't count.

My favourite Maori (an indigenous New Zealander) word is '**Mana**' – pronounced Marrnna. It means presence. When you feel good about yourself you will increase your Mana and you will attract much more success.

6

Buckle Your Seat Belt - Never Charge By a Time Unit

I would love to meet the person who invented 'time based billing'. I think this person is a complete business moron and I would have much pleasure in highlighting the unethical behaviour that this method causes. This is probably the same person who invented 'write-offs' as well. What a complete idiot.

The premise is that if you get the 'charge rate' right and the 'time to do the job' right then the price is right. Nothing could be further from the truth. Time based billing does not value the project. The only value of a project is what the market is prepared to pay for it. In this chapter I will challenge your thinking of time based billing and encourage you to adopt a new model of value pricing.

Time is Not Money

Someone coined the phrase - time is money. What a load of BS. Time is not money. Money is money. A good use of time can turn opportunities into money – but time itself is not money.

Accountants have turned this 'time is money' mantra into a sophisticated art form.

An elaborate system has been created of recording time and then charging the time with a charge rate per hour rather than charging for the value of the work. Seeing how smart accountants are I find that very strange. You might say that the time and rate model does create the true value of the work. I beg to differ. You see, how do you know what your work is really worth? The true determiner of the value of your work is what your client is prepared to pay for it. If the client has a problem that you solve, and the impact of solving it is huge for the client, then they should pay based on the value of the outcome – not by the time taken.

Think of this analogy.

> *A washing machine repair-person comes to your fix washing machine. She takes one look at the machine, pulls out her trusty mallet and hits it in precisely the right spot. The washing machine now works. She writes out an invoice for $200. You ask her to itemise the invoice. So she writes. Parts and materials $1. Knowing where to hit it $199.*

<u>You know where to hit it</u> yet you charge by parts and materials!

Using the above analogy your parts and materials are, accountants time and disbursements. Most accountants have allocated their time to be 6 minute 'units' – so 10 units per hour with each unit having a set price. If the accountants' charge rate is $250 per hour then each unit is theoretically 'worth' $25.

As the accountant is doing the work for a client these 'units' are ticking away in the background. So that means that when a new job is started (typically without the client knowing the final price until after the job is complete), or an existing job is worked on, an electronic clock is keeping score. Theoretically, if the accountant has to do something else not related to the client (like go to the rest room or reply to an internal email) then the clock should be stopped and re-started. I know for a fact that this is not the case. Often, the clients' clock remains active in a lot of cases when personal and company activities are going on.

Let's say you take a phone call from the client (and of course you have stopped the clock on another client) and it takes 15 minutes. Your employer has instructed you to start the clock with every 'matter' on every client. How much time do you put down? Is it 2 ½ units? I highly doubt it. My guess is you put round it up to 3 units. You just ripped the client off!!!

Can your worth really be determined by a 6-minute unit? Does the unit price really set the correct price? What a burden to segment your life into small, compartmentalised amounts. No wonder accountants are looking for the 'quick fix' on everything. You are so time driven that you miss the big picture. This method of determining your worth must surely drive low self-esteem and it must drive you crazy at billing time – I know it promotes the wrong behaviour.

The wrong behaviour with this business model is threefold:
1. Not charging for everything that you do for a client.
2. Being rewarded for taking more time and being inefficient.
3. Not focusing on client needs because you are scared the bill will be too high.

Let's look at each one.

Not charging for everything that you do for a client

Whenever I have a group of accountants in a seminar I ask important questions like: *'Put your hand on your heart and honestly tell me when you do the work for a client, how much time actually hits the clock?'*

I have asked over 5,000 fee earning accountants (employees) this question. The answer is always predictable. If there are 100 in the group there will be 2 or 3 that say 100% (they're lying). There will be 5 or so that say 95%. There will be 10 or so that say 90% and the overwhelming response is around 85% (they tell the truth) - many say 80% or less. The first time I asked this question one of the partners of the firm I was working with (Judy) pulled me aside at lunchtime and said, 'they're stealing from me.'

I don't get this. Your business model says charge by time, yet your employees are making judgment calls at the time of doing the work how much the work is worth. Last time I looked it was not your employees business!

I was on the way to golf one day and I called Susan who was the Client Manager with my old accountant. My enquiry was in relation to a new car I was buying for my wife. Susan asked me some questions, gave me the answer and then said 'and if you do it that way you'll have a tax break between $5k and $20k'. She then hung up the phone. It was an 8 minute car ride and the call took 7 minutes of it. Did she give me good customer service? You might say so, because she answered my question. I have to tell you I had no idea what she said – yet she gave me (potentially) $5k to $20k worth of value. I enquired with Peter (Partner at the

firm) how much I was charged for this call. You guessed it. Zero.
It didn't even make the time recording system.

To value her expertise and give me better service, here is how the call should have been handled.

Rob: 'I am going to buy a new BMW for my wife – what is the best way to finance it?'

Susan: 'It sounds like you are driving so I was wondering if this is an urgent matter?'

Rob: ' No – not urgent. I am on the way to golf.'

Susan: 'OK then. The best way to handle this is I need to ask you a whole series of questions and then I will write you a detailed letter of advice that you can take to the finance person. The letter will spell out exactly the best way to finance the vehicle and exactly what you need to do. Depending on your answers you will get anywhere between $5k to $20k tax break on the purchase. So that you can be completely focused I would like to set up a telephone meeting with you (for about 10 minutes) later today when you get back from golf. As I said, you will be able to get between a $5k and $20k tax benefit when you do it the way I tell you to do it. My fee for doing this will be $495 – is that OK with you?'

Rob: 'Sounds great. I'll speak with you at [time].'

Susan: 'I will send you a quick confirmation email now and I will call you at [time].'

After the call Susan can use a standard template (which was used before with another client) with an embedded spreadsheet, send me the letter and now I have something tangible to take to the finance manager at the dealership.

Being rewarded for taking more time and being inefficient

You promote a 'productivity' target to your accountants. The way you typically define productivity is 'client charged time as a percentage of available time'. Most Accountants work on a 37½ hour week and 45 weeks for the year – so available time of 1687 hours. Normally this productivity figure is around 80% of the 1687 hours – or 1350 of client charged hours per year per accountant.

This focus on productivity causes accountants to go slower, make mistakes, inflate the time taken on time sheets, work longer hours (so your team can get their targets), hoard work and not care too much about the client. You are actually rewarded for doing the wrong things.

The right thing to do is to get the job done quickly and accurately for the client. Under this productivity-driving model why would you do that – you'll get less revenue.

With a focus on productivity (selling time) you have inadvertently set up a *'labour for hire'* business. The more labour you get the more revenue you will get. However, this does not drive profitability. What happens with the productivity-driving model is you end up with far too many people to do what work you have to do.

You are not in a labour for hire business – you are in the knowledge selling business. You turn your intellectual capital (what you know) into intellectual property, which is tangible. Your intellectual property comes in the form of letters, reports, spreadsheets, emails, diagrams, manuals and plans.

If you adopt a **pricing up front** model and a **focus on driving time** down then you will run out of standard work. This is a good thing. You can downsize your team, increase your client base and sell additional services to existing clients without adding to your cost structure. When we work with our coachingclub clients and have them adopt this model 100% of them run out of work in the first year. Typically what took the firm 12 months to do last year they do in 9-10 months the first year they adopt the new model. In year 2 they typically do the same work in 6-8 months.

Not focusing on client needs because you are scared the bill will be too high

As a seminar attendee (Client Manager) said to me: '*I want to get out and find out what clients need. I want to sell. I am unable to because the partners want me to have 80% productivity*'.

I think that sums up the entire issue here. It's a conflict.

If you are focused on charging the client for everything then you will miss out on really helping the client with what they need. This behaviour does not encourage relationship building. I think it is a self-esteem issue. You seem to be more comfortable just 'charging time' for the reactive work, rather than really finding out what the client needs – and proactively helping them. I find that most accountants think that the price will be too high (self-esteem again) and the client will not pay the higher fee.

You have to get to the point where you do not have to charge for everything. Your projects should have enough margins in them that you do not have to worry. You should not be charging for quick phone calls or emails. If the clients know that you charge for everything then they will only do the bare necessities with you. They will limit the number of calls they make and the meetings will be efficient but very little time will be allocated to relationship building. The client is constantly thinking, *'I hope I am not getting charged for the time he is asking about my family and the dog – I wish he would just get on with it.'* How can you build a relationship with a client when the client is thinking this?

All interactions with a client are opportunities to discover additional needs. Many phone calls are 'intellectual property selling opportunities' in disguise. You need to train yourself and your team to look for them – and not charge for the time used in finding out what the client needs.

As the world renowned author on professional services firms, David Maister once said: *"What you do with your chargeable time will determine your income. What you do with your non chargeable time will determine your future."*

With this focus on time, another wastage phenomenon occurs – **write-offs!**

What typically happens is the project is worked on by the accountant and when it comes time to draft the bill, the **gutless partner** 'writes down' (discounting before billing) the value of the work. What a self-esteem destroyer. Your accounting team does the best job they can and by way of our actions you tell them they are not worthy. The partners think the client will not pay the full price – how do you know that? Sure, from time to time an accountant 'stuffs up' or there was more work in the project than first thought. If there was more work in the project then you should have communicated this to the client during the work in progress and invoked a 'change order' on the original engagement letter. Oh, I forgot. You did not price the job up front. You'll have to wear the write-off in that case.

Write-offs are one of the easiest things to fix. It's a decision. You decided to write-off. You can decide to write on. Here's how you eliminate write-offs once and for all. This piece of advice is worth millions of dollars.

1. Make a decision to stop writing-off.
2. Price every job up front with client sign-off.
3. Drive time down and take the write up.

It's that simple. Be warned though. If your business model is charging in arrears and you 'write up' a client's work then you have been very unethical. I do not care if you were super efficient, your business model said charge for the time that was taken. There have been many cases of accountants going to court for overbilling. Take a look at the movie 'The Firm' starring Tom Cruise. In the last scene the law firm was brought unstuck for overbilling. These are write-ups using a time based, price in arrears model.

I have said it before, and I'll say it again. You are doing your clients a complete disservice by focusing on charging them for everything and not building relationships with them.

To sum it up, how can this time and rate model ever work when…

a) The price per hour is based on an accountants' salary level.
b) The time to do the job is never properly recorded.
c) The time taken varies from person to person.
d) You are rewarded for taking longer and being inefficient.

If you are going **to be completely ethical** and true to your time based business model then you should be charging by the hundredth millionth of a second not a 6 minute unit.

I think this entire method of pricing by time is not only bad for you it is bad for your client. It is highly unethical. There is no winner. There has to be a better way. The good news is, there is a better, more ethical way.

It's called Value Pricing.

It's all about working with the client to scope and then price each project based on what value the client gets out of the project. You price the project so there is fair and equitable remuneration for you and a dramatic return on investment for the client. You do this before you commence work on the project. You then communicate in writing the scope, price and value to the client and then get the client to approve the project.

Charge Rates and Value Pricing

It's like the old saying, 'blue and green should never be seen'. The same goes with charge rates and value pricing – they do not go together.

How can you really value price a project if in the back of your mind there is a charge rate hanging over your head. You will constantly struggle with the charge rate and not focus on the value of the work.

So get rid of the charge rates - all of them! Once you start pricing all jobs up front, they are surplus to requirements.

Be warned though. Do not get rid of charge rates until you are pricing every project up front. I would advise that you initially keep time sheets (and put the charge rate at $1 per hour per person) for measurement purposes however as soon as you are comfortable with the strategy and highly profitable, eliminate time sheets as well.

Once you get rid of charge rates you can have this wonderful conversation with a client or prospect when they ask you, **"What are your charge rates?"**

*Just about every accounting firm in the country uses charge rates.
Those firms that use them are directly rewarded for how inefficient they are. The longer they take the more they get. In our view*

*that is unethical behaviour. We don't think that is fair on you so
here at XYZ we don't use charge rates. Instead, we will give you
a fixed price for the work that we undertake. You will receive
that price in writing and in advance of us starting. When we get
into the work if we are inefficient then that's our problem – the
price remains the same. If the scope of the work changes as we
get into the project then we will inform you of any price changes.
Normally the price does not change because we spend quality time
with you at the outset to determine the exact scope of the work.
Overall we think this is a fairer way to do business.'*

You just promoted how your firm is different and more client-focused and at the same time you gave every one of your potential competitors a 'back hander'.

*When my son, Hugh, was 12 he asked if there were some jobs he
could do at the office. I told him I needed 1000 stickers adhered to
1000 paper bags. He said, 'How much will you pay me?' I said
10 cents a unit. 'Is that 10 cents for the bag and the sticker?' he
asked. Smart kid. 'No – 10 cents per completed item.' On the first
morning he did 200 bags in 3 hours and I gave him $20. He
was thrilled. I told him he made about $7 per hour and then I
said when you come back next week to finish the remaining 800
do you want to be paid 10 cents per unit or $7 per hour. As quick
as a flash he said, "10 cents a unit – I'll probably do it faster next
week".*

If a 12 year old gets it then what is your problem! Never charge by the hour. It'll send you to the poor house.

Moving to Value Pricing

The idea of value pricing is that your clients know how much the price will be before the work commences and you get a healthy margin in return for your intellectual capital / property.

With the implementation of value pricing your 'average hourly rate' (AHR) should increase dramatically. There are 2 ways to measure AHR.

The first is if you have time sheets then it is: **Revenue / client hours charged**. So if your revenue was $3M and your fee earning team (including partners) did 10,000 client charged hours for the year then your AHR would be $300.

Once you get rid of time sheets you gain a new value priced focus but lose some of your measurement metrics. You can however measure AHR based on your total employee base. The equation becomes: **Revenue / total working time**. So if your revenue was $3M and you had 10 people (total team including partners) who were paid for 1687 hours for the year then your total working time is 16,870 hours. That would mean your AHR without time sheets is $178.

The objective is to increase your AHR every month – or as a minimum every quarter. At the time of writing, most firms start their journey with time sheets and an AHR around the $150 mark. Our coachingclub program is designed to triple your starting figure as quickly as possible – without tripling the price your client pays.

There are 6 logical steps to increase your margins as illustrated in the model below. As you move through the steps your AHR should be going through the roof.

Margin progression

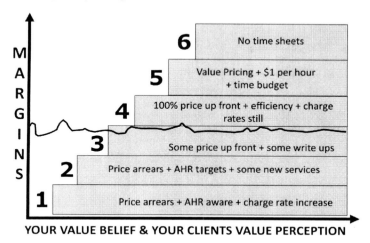

Your margins will increase based on 3 key factors:

1. Your value belief in yourself and the project – courage and self-esteem.

2. Your clients' value perception – how much value they perceive they get.

3. The tactics and strategies you adopt – the 6 steps implemented.

I am going to deal with no. 1 & no. 2 in the next segment of 'setting the price'. For now I want to focus on the tactics and strategies as you quickly move up the margin ladder.

You will notice that there is a 'waterline' half way through the strategies. If you are operating below the waterline you will be drowning in margin poverty. If you are above the waterline you will be surviving in margin abundance.

As you understand each step do not be concerned that you have to take one step after another. You can jump steps and go right to level 5 or 6. You need to get above the drowning point as quickly as possible. The faster you get to the top, the higher your margins will be.

Step 1. Price arrears + AHR aware + charge rate increase

Most firms start here. They price in arrears with time sheets and they are aware of their AHR. They may not be happy with where the AHR is but it is where it is. To increase your margin simply put your charge rates up. Put them all up by 15%. Do that today. No one will notice and make sure you do not adjust salaries at the same time. If you do 10,000 client hours and your AHR was $150 and now with a price rise of 15% it is now $172.50 you just made an additional $225,000 profit. I knew I should have value priced this book!

Step 2. Price arrears + AHR targets + some new services

You are still pricing in arrears (with an increased charge rate) and now you have an AHR target. The price rise got you to $172.50 AHR and now you might set an initial target of $200. To get to a higher target you may need to introduce some more valuable services that are worth more to your clients and more to you – such as business advisory or management accounting services. As you move through the levels keep having a higher and higher AHR target, however be warned. Once you get into value pricing the focus cannot be on the AHR target because you will start to price services based on the target – rather than the value of the project. You are still drowning in margin poverty.

Step 3. Some price up front + some write-ups

You have gone through the first 2 steps and now you have 'put your toe in the water' and tested some upfront pricing on some clients. The clients are always happy and as a result of this you inadvertently become more efficient and you get some write-ups. You are just starting to put your head above the drowning line and heading towards margin abundance. However it's a bit like being pregnant with this price up front strategy. You can't be half pregnant and you can't be half doing this strategy – you either are or you are not.

Step 4. 100% price up front + efficiency + charge rates still

Now you're starting to move into margin abundance. You have committed to price _every_ project up front and now you are really driving time down by being more efficient. Your margins are climbing, your write-offs are eliminated for good and you are getting through the work much faster. You'll be running out of work soon – be prepared. You are still holding onto charge rates. While you still have charge rates, your internal budget will be based on a dollar figure which the team will achieve ('you have $X worth of time to do the job') and you will set the price based on your AHR target or based on charge rates – albeit they are higher than before.

Step 5. Value pricing + $1 per hour + time budget

It's now time to get rid of the charge rates and the AHR targets. If you get rid of the charge rates and move to (initially) $1 per hour per person you will be less inclined to price based on time but on the value of the project. You can still measure and monitor what is going on because you have not eliminated the time sheet recording system – yet! When you do an internal team budget (for the project) you should do it in hours not dollars and the team cannot associate the time taken with the price the client has agreed to pay. You should always challenge the time and drive it down by being more efficient. Your team is even more inclined to record all the time and you'll get an accurate AHR. Your write-offs were eliminated in step 4 – you will only achieve write-offs in step 5 if you are REALLY inefficient. Every firm that has gotten to step 5 will never go back to having charge rates. They are redundant and surplus to requirements.

Step 6. No time sheets

The step every accountant wants to take but is scared to take! Getting rid of the timesheets. The tyranny of time will finally be lifted when you do. However, be warned. Many firms have eliminated time sheets too early. I think it is a sensible option, and one that you will not regret. You should do it when the time is right. I know of some firms that have eliminated time sheets too early and they have nearly gone broke in the process. I know of some firms that have eliminated time sheets and not priced jobs up front – they literally made up the price after the fact. What a mess. I know of firms that have eliminated time sheets and have had a blowout of people costs. I think the time to eliminate time sheets is when your AHR with time sheets is already high (say more than $300), your turnaround time on jobs is fast (say less than 2 weeks) and your profit margin is already high (around the 50% mark before partner salaries). Once you get rid of time sheets some of your measurement systems go as well. This is not a bad thing. Your main KPI's now become profit, turnaround time (not WIP), debtors and AHR (based on revenue / total working time). It certainly simplifies things and saves a huge amount of time filling the darn things in.

These steps are there to be jumped. Get to level 6 as quickly as you can and you'll never look back.

To make all of this happen you should announce your new intentions to your clients. Be bold and send them a letter that reads something like this:

Dear [client],

Since our firm was started in [year] we have been using a 'time multiplied by rate per hour' method to determine the price of the work. Nearly every accounting firm worldwide uses this method.

We have come to the realisation that this method is an archaic method of pricing. It is also a conflict of interest because what it means is (as an industry) we are directly rewarded for how inefficient we are. The longer we take to do the job the more we get. It is not promoting good customer service of faster completion time. This also means you have no idea how much the job will be until the bill is received. We don't think that is fair on you. As a courtesy to you we think you deserve to know in advance how much the job will cost and what it entails. As a modern & progressive firm we have decided to change this 'old' business practice as of [date]. This means that before every job starts we will advise how much it will cost. There will be a written communication that you will need to sign off on. If you are uncertain about the project, the price or the benefits, you will have the opportunity to discuss these with us at the outset. To get the new system up and running, we are clearing out all of the time which we have accumulated to date on your behalf under the old system. Accordingly, please find enclosed an invoice, which brings you right up to date. Other than for minor incidentals that we attend to from time to time, this is the last time you will receive such an invoice from us. We are indeed bringing in a bold new era for accountants. We appreciate your business very much and are confident that this new method of pricing will enable us to give you far better service. We look forward to working with you under the new arrangement.

Yours sincerely,

[Partner name]

By sending this letter, you have cleaned out your work in progress in one go and you have just made yourself accountable to the strategy.

Setting the Price

The most popular question I get is, 'how do you determine the price?' Unfortunately, there is no easy answer to that. If you were in the commodity business (selling the same things that others sell) then it would be relatively easy – see what your competitors are selling their comparable product for and price yours higher or lower based on the quality of your product and service.

You are not in the commodity business – unless of course your business is personal income tax returns and you are competing against the 'sandwich board' style tax agents on the sidewalk. They market personal income tax returns as a commodity with a low price and as such they have 'commoditised' the service.

With a commodity you can have a major differential in price depending on the circumstances. Take a 600ml bottle of water for example. In the supermarket, in a pack of 12 or 24, the water retails for around 60c each. The same water at the convenience store retails for around $2.50. The same water at the airport retails for $4 and in the 5 star hotel mini bar it retails for $5 – or more. Scarcity and circumstances can drive price.

Your products are unique. Your products are based on what you know. You turn <u>your</u> (and your firm's) intellectual capital into intellectual property. You do not sell a commodity service and you have no true competitors – because no one is you. Yes there are many other accounting firms who sell compliance, business advisory and consulting services. Yet you are unique with your special blend of relationship and customer service.

So if that is the case, then the only determiner of your product price is what the market is prepared to pay for it. This means you need to test different packages and approaches to see what your market is prepared to pay for your product. It means you need to listen to what the market is saying (do they have fee questions or fee objections) and re-price or re-package accordingly. It means you cannot dictate to the market what they are prepared to pay. That would be extremely arrogant. Yet under the 'time x rate' model that's exactly what you do. You tell (rather than listen) the market what they will pay.

So if you adopt a new model of listening to your market then that means you need to adopt a new model of testing. Here's an example:

I received an email from one of our coachingclub members (Sean), which was titled 'win for the day'. Sean is the business manager of an extremely successful accounting firm – they have won our coveted 'Accounting Firm of the Year' Award twice in the past 4 years. The story was about one of the partners (Marc) who was about to go into a client meeting. Before he went into the meeting Sean asked Marc to role-play what he was going to say, how he was going to say it and what he was thinking of charging the client. Marc explained his case to Sean and said 'I am thinking of $25k for the project'. Sean says 'I would be prepared to pay $45k for it. And when you get to telling them the price do not say 'umm' in front of the price – say it with confidence'. By simply speaking with someone else before getting to the price, Marc now had a different perspective on what the job was worth. So Marc gets into the meeting, explains the opportunity to the client and of course the client says, 'How much will it *cost?' Marc says (with great tonality and confidence) – 'The fee will be $50k.' The client said yes without hesitation! The email continues – 4 years ago before we joined coachingclub we would have charged around $5K.*

I saw Marc a few weeks after receiving the email and I asked him specifically (when the price was mentioned) what the client said and how the client said it. *Marc said at the time he mentioned the price, the client put both thumbs up and said, 'That's an excellent use of money.'*

The client said yes without hesitation. The price was probably wrong! Could Marc have gotten $60k or $70k for the project? Probably. Was Marc ecstatic with what he got – you bet.

There is no right or wrong price. However, if your clients are continually saying 'yes' to your price, then the price is wrong. The right price is just before lots of 'noes'.

Put the price up and **let the marketplace tell you** when you've gone far enough. If you push the boundaries and you get lots of 'noes' then back it off a bit and settle on a price that has a great margin for you and a good return for the client.

Your price is determined by 2 factors only.

1. Your value belief in yourself and the project – your courage and self-esteem.
2. Your clients value perception – how much value they perceive they are getting.

Here is a great example of value belief. In my live seminars I will often have the accountants tell me how much they have charged for certain projects. This one is a standard project that most accountants have done and one that invokes some interesting prices.

How much have you charged in the past for this service?

I have everyone write down what they have charged in the past for
this service. The results are staggering. The current low price is $500
and the current high price is $30K – and everywhere in between. A 60
times variable for the same instructions!

There have been 2 accountants at $30K, 3 at $25K and hundreds
around the $10K mark. I asked one of the accountants (Chris) who
had charged $30K, why so much? Chris' response: *'Without us they
cannot get the loan – that's our value add!'*

WOW – now there is an accountant who understands his value.
Who am I to tell you how much to charge when there is a 60 times
variable. I have come to the conclusion I know nothing about how
much to charge – I keep putting my prices up and they keep saying
yes.

*Recently I was in a hotel and I was having a massage. I was
paying $150 for the hour-long (above board) service. As I lay
on the massage table I started thinking about accountants – yes
very sad I know. The reason I was thinking about you is because*

here I was happily paying $150 for a service where the effects
would not last more than a day. I started thinking about all
the accounting firms where their average hourly rate is well
below $150 yet the effects of the services they provide often last a
lifetime.

The more you understand what your clients get out of implementing your service and the value you create, the more you will believe you are worth more. Your value belief and self-esteem will improve as will your courage to charge more.

As you go through this journey of value belief and client value perception you have to be conscious of **'price parity'**. If a client has been paying $5K for your service and even if you feel it is worth twice as much, the client may not pay much more for it – particularly if it looks like the same service. Your client might pay 15% or 20% more, but double? – Give me a break. Unless you completely re-design your product offering, so it looks completely different your current client will have a hard time paying the price. When it comes to new services that the client has never bought before – different story. There is no price parity with a new service that has not been purchased before – charge at will!

I received an email from a seminar attendee one day, explaining
that she asked the client, 'What do you think it is worth?' The
client said, 'I don't know – I'll buy you lunch.' The accountant
was thinking $2K!

Do not say it that way. Your language and how you articulate a project will often determine your clients' value perception.

I play a great game with my coaching clients and seminar attendees called, 'Where's the value?' It's all about you articulating the value of what you do. I always start with basic annual compliance and typically the accountants draw a blank on the real value of compliance. After some prodding I get frustrated and I say: **'As a result of understanding and using your compliance product, tell me what it will enable the client to do and tell me how your client can use it.'** Now the real value of the compliance product comes out. They say as a result of understanding and using the product the client can...

- ✓ Make better and more informed management decisions.
- ✓ Increase their credit lines with suppliers.
- ✓ Appease financiers.
- ✓ Get more capital.
- ✓ Value their business.
- ✓ Mitigate risk by increasing insurance levels.
- ✓ Sell their business.
- ✓ Improve the profit in their business.
- ✓ Use it as a basis for cash flow management.
- ✓ Sleep better at night.
- ✓ Have peace of mind that their affairs are looked after.
- ✓ Increase their wealth.
- ✓ Improve their lifestyle.

Amazing amounts of value, in a seemingly 'valueless' product.

Once <u>you</u> understand how the client can use your product or what result the client can realise by implementing it, you will have a much easier job of articulating the value of your product.

At a recent coachingclub meeting I asked the accountants to play the 'where's the value' game and to articulate the value that they had created for a client. Each accountant had to bring a current project to the meeting and tell everyone else what value the client got out of the project. Sheryl turned up with her compliance project and it had 12 points of value attached to it. I told her that was awesome and then she told me that she drew a blank and did not come up with any of them. She confessed that she emailed her client and told them that she wanted to anonymously talk about the client and could the client tell her the value that she created. The client emailed back 12 points of value.

Sometimes you need to ask others what value you create.

One of the reasons that you do not think in a 'value that you create' way is because you are constantly thinking about **activities and inputs instead of results and outputs**. What I mean is you are thinking (and subsequently articulating) about things – 3 of these, 1 of these and 2 of those – rather than what the client gets out of implementing your things.

Take the diagram below. On the left is a list of typical 'things' that accountants do. They are all valid and noble services. When you just promote these activities and inputs they have no perceived value at all to your client. It's just a shopping list on an engagement letter. When you articulate your language so that your clients understand what they get out of your inputs (right hand side) then they start to realise the true value that you create. And so do you.

Selling what?

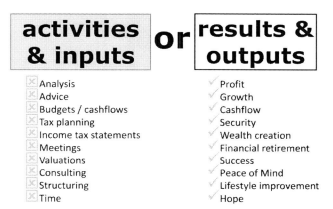

activities & inputs	or	results & outputs
☒ Analysis		✓ Profit
☒ Advice		✓ Growth
☒ Budgets / cashflows		✓ Cashflow
☒ Tax planning		✓ Security
☒ Income tax statements		✓ Wealth creation
☒ Meetings		✓ Financial retirement
☒ Valuations		✓ Success
☒ Consulting		✓ Peace of Mind
☒ Structuring		✓ Lifestyle improvement
☒ Time		✓ Hope

Spend more time speaking in a language that the client understands – what's in it for me – rather than in a language that you understand. If there was a magic formula this might be it.

To settle on a price work out what tangible results a client gets from using your service, work out (by asking them) what other intangible benefits they will receive, then settle on a price that is a good return for you (based on your value contribution and the intellectual capital you bring to the table) and a dramatic return on investment for your client.

To summarise this chapter there are 11 critical things you need to do to get rid of time-based billing and move to a value-pricing model.

1. Realise and believe your services are worth more.

2. Find the courage to charge more.

3. Increase all prices immediately.

4. Offer additional services at the time of buying.

5. Have set prices for repetitive tasks – a standard menu of services and price list.

6. Price in advance not arrears.

7. Articulate the value of each project eloquently.

8. Get rid of low margin services and low margin clients.

9. Improve your language and sales skills.

10. Target more profitable clients & services.

11. Use value based fees – not time X rate!

When you adopt these methods your profits (and enjoyment levels) will improve out of sight. The diagram below shows you the impact of this model using a very small client who has been paying $5K for basic compliance services. Follow the diagram left to right.

Profit improvement

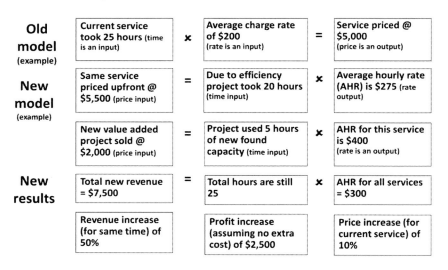

Once you follow this model you will never look back. Your clients will be much happier and so will your bank account.

7

Accountants Make Great Sales People

Think of the <u>most successful</u> sales people you know. If you were to list their traits and characteristics then I would imagine that this list would apply.

1. Ethical
2. Problem solver
3. Personable
4. Trustworthy
5. Good communicator
6. Persistent

7. Passionate

8. Good product knowledge

9. Service focused

10. Good listener

Who am I am talking about here? It is the direct traits of the modern day accountant. Sure some accountants do not openly display their 'passion' however I do know that some are having a party on the inside!

Accountants make great sales people because they have the inherent traits right now. What you are missing is a process. This chapter will demystify sales and introduce you to a sales process that works.

Marketing is Not Sales

Accountants are not very good at marketing – marketing people are. My definition of marketing is '**salesmanship multiplied**'. My definition of sales is '**finding out what the other person needs and then transferring emotion**'. These definitions mean that marketing is a 'one to many' strategy and sales are a 'one on one' strategy.

Marketing is a leveraged activity – such as seminars. Writing, emails, letters and sales are not a leveraged activity. You can certainly 'sell from stage' in a leveraged way at a seminar but what you are really doing is generating leads so you can speak with the prospects at a later date.

Every accounting firm that has serious growth plans needs to hire full-time marketing people. The job of the marketing team (or initially a singular person) is to enhance your company brand – make you look good – and to generate enquiries from your existing and future clients base. Branding and leads – that's all. Make sure that your marketing person(s) are capable of doing this.

Your marketing team might start with a 'Marketing Coordinator' and you may end up with a full time 'Marketing Manager' and a small team that directs the marketing strategy of your business.

The role of your marketing team is to:

- ✓ Manage your prospect database – add to it and keep it up to date with all contact details.
- ✓ Manage your client database – see above.
- ✓ Liaise with outside branding people to keep the image fresh.
- ✓ Coordinate your regular newsletter.
- ✓ Manage your website – freshness, words etc.
- ✓ Liaise with your 'centres of influence' and referral sources.
- ✓ Edit and prepare your articles for distribution.
- ✓ Manage your social media presence - blog, facebook, twitter etc.
- ✓ Send out press releases, email blasts and mailers etc.
- ✓ Organise and manage events – breakfast seminars, boardroom briefings, prospect luncheon meetings, cocktail receptions, seminars, webinars, tele-seminars, conferences etc.
- ✓ Book & manage nurturing visits (with existing clients) for the partners to turn up to.
- ✓ Generate X number of leads per month using the above strategies.

The entire list above is leveraged activities. Outside of the administration aspects of marketing the best marketing people know how to sell. If your marketing people are good at selling then the words that they use (and how they use them) will have a great impact at generating leads.

Often an accounting practice will look around the team and see who has a flair for marketing – and put them in the role. NO accounting businesses will hire professionals who know what they are doing into the roles.

When hiring marketing people make sure their primary focus is on generating leads. Marketing people are great at spending money on 'awareness' and 'image' type campaigns that do not generate any leads at all. They need measurement metrics (just like everyone else in your business does) to go by and the best one (key performance indicator) is 'number of leads generated' each month.

Members of my communities (coachingclub and Proactive Accountants' Network) are hiring marketing people who are using our position descriptions all the time with great results. Just like any position, you do not always get it right the first time. Persevere with the strategy, pay the right amount of money and find the best people you can to market your business – you'll be glad you did.

Accounting is Selling

Sales people typically have a bad image around the world. Even the word 'sales' can make a lot of accountants cringe with distaste. The reason often is because you associate 'salespeople' with words like: dishonest, unethical, convincing, unprofessional, high pressure and fast talker!

Make no question many salespeople are like that. However, they will not be that successful at sales if they stay like that.

After more than 25 years successfully selling all sorts of products and services I think that being successful at sales is all about *finding out what the other person needs and then transferring emotion*.

That means you need to **ask the right questions**. You need to actively **listen**. You need to show **empathy**. You need to **solve problems**. You need to have **product knowledge**. You need to really **believe in your product**. You need to be **ethical**. You need to be **personable**. You need to **promote** your product so the other person gets excited by it. You need to be **persistent** if you believe it is the right thing for the client.

It sounds a lot like being a good accountant!

What do you do every day as an accountant? You find client issues and you solve them. Every day you are doing this. It's the same with being successful at sales. You find what your clients need and then you convey the benefits of them buying what they need to buy.

To be successful at sales you have to proactively speak with people. That means you have to get out from behind your desk and go and visit people or meet with people who would be classed as a qualified enquiry. To do that you need to shake out of what I am calling **'limiting sales beliefs'**. It's all the 'mind chatter' that goes on when you are confronted with the reality that to serve your clients properly you need to make some sales.

The following diagram is a great example of some of the 'chatter' that goes on with most accountants. I am sure you can relate to some (or maybe all) of them.

Limiting Sales Beliefs

Remember this.

- ✓ You can be good at sales if you have the inclination.
- ✓ Yes you are busy but there is nothing more important than properly serving your clients.
- ✓ You will come back with more work – more valuable work for your clients.
- ✓ Your clients do not know what they do not know – you are the finance expert not them.
- ✓ Your clients do not have everything they need – they don't know what they need.
- ✓ What the clients think is none of your business – it's there's.
- ✓ They will say no from time to time – every no is closer to a yes.
- ✓ If you act ethically in the sales process you will be seen as a professional.

As a professional accountant you have lots to offer your clients – you have to believe that. Your job is to have relationships with your clients, to increase the average fee per client, and to win new business. You must ensure all of your clients' needs are met. You just need to get comfortable in talking with people to find out what they need.

How to Be a Guru in Sales

Accountants can be really good at sales – with 'guru like' status.

If you have the inclination, being successful at sales is a skill that you can learn. It involves scripts, dialogues, practice, asking questions and following a sales process.

The first thing to remember with sales is why people buy professional services – particularly services over and above compliance-based services. Your value added professional services.

Most accountants think that it is the quality of the product, the methodology, the content or the process of delivering the work that really turns the client on. Wrong! Only about 10% of the buying decision is based on this. And guess what most accountants (before they are professionally trained) spend most of their time discussing? You guessed it. They spend most of the conversation on product related discussion. They seem to want to talk on and on about the quality of their product, the qualifications of their people, how unique their methods are and how they will work with the client. Clients do not care about this as much as you do.

What clients are interested in (40% of the buying decision) is that you are likeable, trustworthy, you know what you are talking about and they can (or do have) a good relationship with you. Remember, people buy from people. Are your clients and prospects comfortable buying from you?

Even more importantly than your likeability (around 50% of the buying decision) your clients and prospects are most interested in what they get out of the transaction. They are wondering how your ideas will help them improve their results. They are wondering if your service will help them reach their objectives and what they are motivated to achieve.

Reasons why people buy professional services

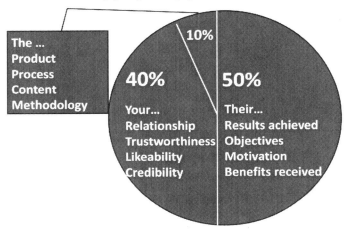

The ...
Product
Process
Content
Methodology

10%

40%

Your...
Relationship
Trustworthiness
Likeability
Credibility

50%

Their...
Results achieved
Objectives
Motivation
Benefits received

Ultimately what accountants sell is the same as what the cosmetics companies sell – **HOPE**. Clients hope that by buying your services you can help them achieve what they want to achieve. Your clients do not understand the intricacies of how you will do the work – nor do they need to.

Spend your discussion time getting your clients to talk about them. Not you talking about you!

As well as focusing on the right areas in your discussions there are 2 key success factors in being successful at sales.

1. Your sales process.

2. Your conversion rate process.

Sales Process – You Need One!

A sales process is the sequence of steps that happen one after another in a systematic and repeatable way. For example what happens when an enquiry comes in? Do you send them some information immediately? Do you book a meeting the same day? What is the script to book the meeting? What happens after the meeting? Do you send an engagement letter the same day or 3 days later? Do you meet again and how quickly after the first meeting? You need a sales process that each person in your business follows consistently.

The number 1 key performance indicator for sales people is the **number of sales meetings** that they conduct. You need to work out how many meetings your team can conduct. I call this your 'quality meeting capacity' - your QMC. If a sales meeting takes on average 2 hours (with travel) and there are 1600 hours per year available per person who is in sales then each salesperson (at maximum productivity) can do around 800 quality meetings. Most of your sales people (Partners and client managers) will be doing some delivery (doing the work) as well, so you have to take that into consideration. You have an enormous amount of sales meeting capacity – how many sales meetings as a firm are you doing?

Many meetings are a waste of time because you are not speaking with people who can make a decision (you MUST be speaking with all the decision makers at the same time, otherwise you are wasting your time) or your decision maker(s) are just fishing around for information. You must quickly qualify who you are speaking with and what their time frame is for buying. You can do many sales meetings however if the meetings are just 'nice' then you'll have no traction – but you will be busy.

With the best of intentions when accountants are in a sales role they say things like 'it's an absolute certainty that this client will spend

$X and the sale will close by [date]'. The date comes around and you guessed it. No sale. They do not mean to tell lies – but they do. All sales people tell lies. The reason is because there is no accurate forecasting and pipeline management system. The probability of a sale should be based on the stage (steps in the process) of the sale. So an initial consultation might be 25%, a second meeting 50%, an implementation plan sent 75%, a verbal yes 90% and money in the bank – 100%. The date of closure should be based on when the client tells you it will close – which means you need to ask timing questions and let the client tell you when they want to do business. Never assume.

In your sales process you need written meeting agendas, a question sequence to follow and you need to record the major parts of the conversation. If you write down the major points of the conversation and you manage that through a database management (often called CRM) system you will be able to deal with more prospects at one time. When I have been in a full time sales role selling professional services (average fee around $30k) I would typically manage around 100 prospects at any one time. Being organised enables you to do this.

Finally, whatever your sales process is, you need to set targets and monitor the success of the process and each person who follows it. Once you work out each person's QMC get the sales person to tell you how many meetings they will do. Some people will have a higher close rate (prospect to sale ratio) or the time to make a sale (number of days the opportunity is open) will be less. Others will have a higher average transaction per sale. Find out what these people are doing, have them train the rest and replicate it over and over again.

Conversion Rate Process

Just doing more meetings is a good start. Once you have people actually meeting prospects and clients you will go a long way to making sales.

As you monitor the conversion rate of each person (prospect to sale ratio), the number of meetings it takes to make a sale and the average sale value that you need, to work on improving each area. You are looking for a higher conversion rate and fewer meetings per sale at a higher average transaction value per sale.

One of the key ingredients to sales success is the individuals' self-belief and conviction – it comes across as confidence and passion. You need to get more of it. Just like a dog can smell fear so too can a prospect. If you have a speech impediment this will affect your success. If you perspire a lot from your armpits or on the palms of your hands this will affect your success. If you say 'ummm' before sentences this will affect your success. If you look like an unkempt slob this will affect your success. If you do not seem confident in your tone this will affect your success. You may need to 'fake it until you make it' during your sales conversations. Take a deep breath before you get into the meeting. Wear dark clothing – and don't raise your arms. Wipe your hand on a cloth in your pocket before shaking hands. Invest in some new threads that make you feel better. Get some speech coaching. You need to think like a duck on a lake – cool and calm on top but paddling like heck underneath. You need to get those butterflies flying in formation!

During your sales conversation, your number one goal should be to find your clients' motivation. You need to find out what their objectives are, what problems they are looking to solve, what their goals are and what they want to achieve by using your services. You need to practice the types of questions you will ask. You need to role-play with colleagues before you meet the client. You need to use words and sentences that are conducive to finding out what your clients objectives are (see 'the language of the sale' coming up next) and you need to do a 'needs analysis' with each client. Our coachingclub clients and network members use T.R.U.S.T (The Really Useful Selling Tool) – to electronically find client / prospects needs.

I love educating prospects during a sales process. That means they have learned something about their situation during the sales process. When you offer a 'taster' of advice during the sales process you are consulting to them whilst selling. An example is that you could tell your clients / prospect what to do, but not how to do it. During the process of selling I like to use a strategy, which I have perfected called 'what if' selling. That means that you focus on '**now**' numbers (broken down by key performance indicators in the profit & loss and balance sheet) and based on you helping the client (you tell them how you can help them) there is a hypothetical '**where**' result in each of the KPI's that the prospect nominates. Once extrapolated, the difference in profit, cash, wealth is always massive. Makes your fees look insignificant and a great return on investment.

What you send to your clients / prospects during the process (you may have multiple meetings) will have an impact on your success. You should be citing case studies and testimonials of other successful clients you have worked with. You should be sending follow up cards, emails and other items of interest. Your implementation plans (you would typically call these proposals or engagement letters) should be a confirmation device that summarises your conversation. They should follow the 'language of the sale' process and cover no more than 4 pages.

There should not be an objection that you have not heard before. You should have a great answer for each objection. You should have a standard objection and answer list. Once you get an objection (and you will get plenty of them) the best way to handle them is to use the 'feel, felt, found' technique. Here's an example: 'I know how you **feel**, others that we have done this for **felt** exactly the same before we got started. What they **found** was that once we implemented this solution they ... benefit, benefit, benefit.

So you have had a great meeting – now what? Most accountants in a sales role (and unsuccessful salespeople) say things like 'come back to me when you are ready' or 'let me know if you are interested'. Arrgh – you just poured cold water on the sale. You've had a good meeting so always remember the true objective of the meeting – to book the next steps. You should always BAMFAM. You should always **book a meeting from a meeting**. You need to progress the sale with the next step. The next step could be a follow up meeting, an implementation plan sent or a start date. Either way there is an event that happens after every sale. Systematically book it every single time after every single meeting.

If all else fails simply ask for the business. Literally, 'Do you want to achieve what we have outlined and when do you want to achieve that?' They can only say NO. If you have done the best job you can in the process, you have uncovered their objectives and you have followed up in a timely manner then remember they are only saying NO to themselves and their objectives – not you. As my sales manager (Perry) says – 'every no is closer to a yes'. It's not your problem.

The Language of the Sale

If you went to a sales training course a few decades ago you would have been educated that 'selling is telling'. That might have been the case when product quality was the key differentiator and to sell your product. You would follow the old formula of F.A.B – features, advantages & benefits. You were taught to talk about the features of your product, talk about the advantages of the product & then finally (after more talking) you would tell the client the benefits of the product. You would talk yourself into the sale and then out of the sale and then into it again until finally the prospect would buy so they could get rid of you! Or they would politely say, 'I need to go away and think about it.' That's a NO.

When I have a group of accountants that I am teaching to sell, I will initially (before the skills are taught) give them a role-play to do. The have to pair up, one is the client the other plays the accountant (seller) and they are given a real client scenario to play out. When we do the debrief the standard response was the accountant did all the talking and did not ask that many questions. And you guessed, not too many made a sale.

Then I would demonstrate how it should be done. What I do is select any accountant from the audience and the accountant plays the client – I play the accountant. It has to be a real client that is a typical compliance based client that has some potential. Most of the time the client is paying the firm around $5k - $10k per year. I ask about 60 seconds worth of background questions (that I should know because I am the accountant) and then I set the scene. We are in a neutral place. I am visiting the client for the first time. The client knows the meeting is free. The audience has to observe the meeting and write down any process, questions asked etc. The audience also has to write down potential additional services the client needs to buy to satisfy the client's needs. I tell the audience that this will be an amazing meeting, one of the best they have ever seen and they need to keep completely quiet and it will be so good that we may start to levitate. Off we go with me asking loads of leading questions in a **very particular way**.

I have done this interview (playing the accountant) over 50 times and it always ends in the same way. The client buys with a substantial number of new services. Typically the client will be paying 5 to 10 times more per year with the additional services needed. The meeting format is predictable and teachable. You may never get to witness (or experience) this meeting with me so instead of leaving you hanging, here is my 12 step meeting approach:

Step 1. Make sure all of the decision makers are at the meeting.

Step 2. Set the scene. Why we are having the meeting – the client is wondering.

Step 3. Frame the meeting purpose and time frame of the meeting.

Step 4. Understand the 'now' by asking a series of background related questions.

Step 5. Understand what the clients' goals and objectives are – what they want to achieve.

Step 6. Ask how they would know if they have achieved their objectives.

Step 7. Ask what it would mean to them if we helped them achieve their objectives.

Step 8. Ask what their current plans are to achieve their objectives.

Step 9. Ask what the consequences are of not doing something different.

Step 10. Ask timing related questions – when they want to get started to achieve their objectives.

Step 11. Tell the client the next steps – write a plan to achieve objectives with options to take.

Step 12. Book the next steps – another meeting to clarify details or getting started date.

Leave a step out and the meeting is not predictable – it just does not work as well.

Being a sales success is not about telling. It's about asking open-ended questions and listening. Really listening. My model of 'great questions' below is about asking questions in a sequence. After years of testing, the sequence must be followed to the letter. You will see it follows my 12- step approach to the successful meeting.

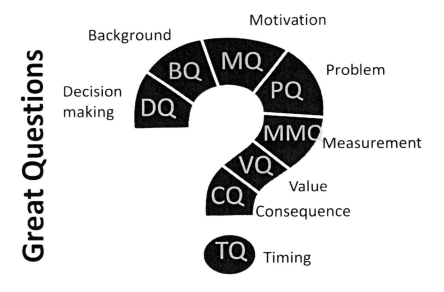

Under each of the categories there are a range of questions you could ask. Work out which ones you are comfortable with and ask them. Then listen, write down the answer and then ask the next one.

DQ's – making sure you are speaking with your buyer. Often you are not speaking with all the people who can make a decision. You need to find the **decision makers** by asking direct questions:

1. *Can you sign off on this plan without speaking with anyone else?*
2. *Who are the owners / directors / shareholders of your business?*
3. *Who else is involved in making this decision?*
4. *Who are the key decision makers in your business?*

BQ's – understanding the **background** of the current situation. You cannot prescribe services until you diagnose the situation. You can ask questions like:

1. *So that I can understand your business fully – can you tell me what are the key things that make it work the way it does?*
2. *If you look back to when you first started / bought your business where did you think it would be today?*
3. *So that I can understand your cash flow situation, can I just ask in what order do you pay the following: Yourself, Creditors, Wages, Tax department?*
4. *What is your overdraft limit and what is the typical cash balance?*
5. *How has the revenue & profit been over the past 3 years – increasing, flat, going backwards? And what do you put that down to?*
6. *If you had your time over again what would you do differently?*

MQ's & PQ's – you need to understand the clients' objectives. Where they want to go, what they want to achieve (**motivation**) and what they want to fix (**problems**). Questions like:

1. *Over and above what you are planning to do – what would be your 'ideal world' business objectives?*
2. *If you could crystal ball your business and your life what would it look like?*
3. *Take the business out 3 years – what would you like it to look like?*

4. *What would you like to achieve by us working together?*

5. *What help do you need from us – and why?*

6. *What has led us to having this meeting – what are you wanting to achieve?*

7. *What are the current issues you would like solved that you are grappling with?*

8. *What is getting in the way of you achieving your objectives right now?*

9. *What are the specific things you want to achieve?*

10. *Why are these objectives important to you?*

11. *How badly do you want to achieve these objectives?*

12. *How confident are you that you will achieve these objectives without our help?*

13. *What other objectives you would like to achieve?*

MMQ's – you and your client need to understand how the project that you are about to propose will be measured. You need **measurement metrics** and the client must state what they are. There is only one question to ask once you have determined the objectives.

1. *We can certainly help you achieve those objectives. They are completely in line with what we do. We've helped many other clients achieve theirs, we enjoy it and we're good at it. So that you know if you have achieved your objectives we will work with you to measure the success of every project. In line with measuring the success, how would __you__ know if we have helped you achieve your objectives?*

VQ's – the **value** that the client receives by implementing your ideas. This is where you start to get emotional buy-in to your project.

1. *We can help you achieve those objectives. As I said we are good at it and we have done it before. If we could help you achieve them what would be the impact on you and the business?*

2. *If we could help you achieve your objectives what would it mean to you and your business?*

3. *If we could help you achieve your objectives what are the main benefits you would realise?*

4. *If we could help you achieve your objectives what significant difference would it make to you and your business?*

CQ's – having your client understand the consequences of not buying your services and doing something different. There are 2 key questions and a statement to make at the end.

1. *What are your current plans that you have in place to help you achieve your objectives?*

2. *What are the consequences if you do not do something different?*

3. *So what you are saying is you have to do something different to achieve your objectives!*

TQ's – **timing** related questions that start to wrap up the meeting. You need to find out when this project is going to start.

1. *What is going to happen from here is I am going to go away and write a detailed implementation plan on how you can achieve your objectives and realise your potential. In the plan it will have an agreed start date, some different implementation options you*

can choose and a set fee for each of the options. (If appropriate)
Any fee charged will be funded out of new cash flow. So that I
can set the start date are there any cyclical dates / trips / scheduled
coming up that I need to be aware of?

2. *Ok - is this a later or a sooner project for you to get started?*

3. *Great. I will check our workflow schedule and put a proposed start*
   date during the week of (date)? How does suit you?

Finally, how to close the meeting and book the next steps – after timing questions.

1. *Great. I will send you the implementation plan by close of*
   business (day), you'll have some questions when you read it and
   we will more than likely need to meet again. When would you get
   a chance to read it?

2. *So could we meet again on (day) at (time) to answer questions*
   and confirm the appropriate option, and then get you started?

3. *So just to confirm. I will send you the implementation plan by*
   close of business (day), you'll read it (over the weekend), and then
   if we can meet again on (day) at (time) we'll go over everything,
   answer questions and get started.

You will notice you are NOT talking about your firm, your people, how good you are or your solutions. The entire conversation is about the client. Their situation and what they want to achieve by hiring you to help them.

For maximum success, here are a couple of sales tips that go with this meeting format:

1. Do not go armed with a long list of questions to ask – you'll get confused. Just remember the process and let it flow.

2. Make sure you have all of the decision makers in the meeting – you are wasting your time otherwise. If you do not have all of the decision makers in front of you, you will need to re-book the meeting.

3. It's a conversation – not an interrogation. Use question softeners before each question.

4. Your tonality will play a part in your success. If you have a weak tone or you mumble then you will not make as many sales.

5. Your enthusiasm is important. Tell the client if they have a good business and make sure you smile.

6. Spend most of your time on the BQs, MQs and PQs.

7. Always, always book the next steps – B.A.M.F.A.M.

8. Remember to have fun. They can only say no.

A game I play with accountants is 'sales rugby'. I gather the accountants in a circle and have one throw the rugby ball to someone who has to pick an objection card from the pack. On one side is the objection – the other the answer. I read the objection and then the accountant has to answer quickly and succinctly.

Here are 3 great ones, which will help you to deal with objections.

Client: How much will this cost?

You: I don't know yet. I need to go away and think about it. I will come back to you with a detailed implementation plan, which will outline some implementation options you could take and each one will have a set fee.

Client: I have no money to pay for it

You: That's exactly why you need me/us! I am serious about this (in a serious and authoritative tone) - name. We need to work with you to sort out your profit and cash flow situation. If we do not help you then you will always be in this situation. You will never be able to realise your potential, your family will not be properly supported and any goals or dreams you have can be kissed goodbye. You will never succeed. We have currently helped X other clients (assuming you have) with exactly the same thing. An example of that is (cite some examples) and they were in exactly the same situation as you. They now are (give examples). Because a cash flow & profit plan is an ongoing project we can structure the payment arrangements on a monthly basis. And typically the fee we charge you will be funded out of new and additional cash flow. We're good at this sort of work, we've done it before and we love doing it. But before we get into the specifics of how we can help you I want to understand your objectives. Assuming we can help you in this area, and we can, what would you like your business to look like in the next 3-5 years?

Client: What is your hourly rate for this sort of work?

You: We do not use hourly rates. Our fees are based on our contribution to the value you receive as a result of the project. We will be fairly rewarded for our contribution and you'll get a tremendous return on your investment.

I have been professionally speaking (getting paid to speak) since 1993 and I have been averaging about 80 presentations per year. I learned a long time ago that you always give 3 speeches, or you give 3 presentations or give 3 meetings.

1. The one you intend on giving.
2. The one you actually give.
3. The one you should have given, that you give to yourself on the way home.

Your meetings, presentations or speeches will never be right. Get over yourself and go do some!

8

Together Everyone
Achieves More

When it comes to sporting success what is better, '*A team of champions*' or a '*championship team*'? You know the answer. A championship team will beat a team of champions every single time. The sporting arena is littered with successes where a team that works well together outperforms the team that has the superstars and big names in the team.

The same with business success. You need a single team working together with the one vision, one plan and the shared passion to achieve your success.

So how do you get everyone on the same page with complete 'buy-in', working together and implementing? This chapter will explore some ideas that you can implement to create a high performing team.

Building a High Performing Team

There are 5 areas to focus on when building a high performing team in an accounting business.

1.   Do you have the right people?
2.   Are they motivated, excited and passionate?
3.   Do they know what to do?
4.   Do they know how to do it?
5.   Is the environment conducive to a high achieving culture?

The Right People

You know if you have the wrong people on your team and to get rid of them would be a great benefit to your business. You know this but you do nothing about it. Why is that? You will always make some mistakes in hiring people and you will always have problems with people – hire one person and you start to have problems! But putting up with the wrong people for so long in your business – that's inexcusable.

With so many people available to be hired, there is no excuse to not have the very best people on your team. If you change your business model you can create additional profitability and afford to have the best people available.

Get rid of the wrong people. The leopard will never change its spots and they will drag your business down. If you have to fire them, performance-manage them out or even make the position redundant then do it.

The right team members need to be selected on attitude first and skills second. You can train the skills – hard to change the attitude.

Excited, Motivated and Passionate

Assuming you have the wrong people off your bus and the right people are on it then you need to make sure they want to be there. Are they doing what they love? Are they motivated to help clients? Are they passionate about their work?

Last time I looked there were 168 hours in a week. How many hours do you think are associated with:

1. Getting ready for work.
2. Getting to work.
3. Actually being at work.
4. Coming home from work.
5. Thinking about work!

My guess is that around 50% of your waking life is associated with work. Half of your (and your team's) adult working, waking life is associated with work. Half your life! I sincerely hope that for the benefit of your clients, your loved ones, your fellow teammates and in particular yourself that you are motivated doing what you do and you enjoy it.

If you do not enjoy what you do then do something else. You're going to spend half your life doing what you're currently doing.

I was in a coachingclub meeting once, talking about doing what you love and an accountant (a sole practitioner called Janice) said, 'I do not enjoy this business. I loathe it. My husband and I have other business interests. I am going to sell it.' The next day she sold the firm to her second in command for $750K in cash.

Knowing What to Do

Do your team members have clear job descriptions, implementation tasks and workflow projects to keep them busy? Do they know what to do on a daily basis? Is it crystal clear what they are working on, what their priorities are and who they are working with? Many accountants I get to meet, run out of work to do – yet the partners are always busy. If the business is well run from a workflow point of view then it should be properly resourced and the team should be kept busy all of the time.

Knowing How to Do It

Let's say you hire a new accountant. They have 8 years experience working for 2 other firms. You are excited to get this fully qualified superstar accountant on your team. You have loads of work to do so the induction process might go like this:

'Hi [name], welcome to the firm. You'll be working in [name's] team. Here is your desk, your computer, your chair, your login and here is a heap of unfinished work to get into. You have 8 years experience so you must know what to do. Let me know your progress on Friday afternoon over a beer. Good luck.'

Just because this superstar accountant has 8 years experience at 2 other firms it does not mean they know how your business works. Have a good look at your induction process and ongoing training process. When someone joins your business, what happens in the first week? Are they properly inducted into your business? What is the ongoing soft skills (not just technical based) training program?

Are your teams enjoying a healthy mix of internal and external training programs? More often than not external training programs provide a better and more cost effective solution.

The Right Environment

If you and your team are going to spend 50% of your working waking life at work then shouldn't the workplace be a great place to be at?

I visit many accountancy offices and I mostly find the environment is not that great. Often I find the furniture is tired, the office is closed and dark, the computer equipment is not up to date, the meeting rooms are untidy, the colours are dated and there is a limited choice of food and beverage available.

You know you have the right environment, if your team members bring their friends to work to show off the premises. Let your team decide what sort of workplace they want. Have a brainstorming session, get them involved and do not put the 'financial editor' on during this process. Do the cost justification and all of the ideas come out.

With a coat of paint, some fresh plants, some new furniture and some fresh ideas you can make any environment look great.

As I observe high performing teams in the business and sporting arena, they have a few things in common:

1. Common Purpose – they are striving for the same purpose.
2. Values & Standards – they have clear performance standards and shared values.
3. Goal Alignment – everyone is shooting for the same goal.
4. Roles, Responsibilities & Priorities – they all know what and when to do things.
5. Open Communication – there is a channel of consistent communication.

6. Participation & Support – they get involved and support each other.

7. Plan of Action – there is a plan of action that is followed.

8. Risk Taking & Innovation – calculated and innovative risks are taken.

9. Celebration – there is constant celebration like sales bells, recognition and plenty of parties!

Just like you can change your business model to be more profitable you can also re-design how your team works. It's your choice.

A Growth Culture

What is a culture? Think back to your high school science days. A culture is a growth. It's a living organism. Just like a business culture. If your culture is not a growing based culture then it is a dying culture.

Most accountancy firms have a culture but it was not created – it just happened. And what it is today is what it is. If you want to have a high performing business then you need a culture that matches your objectives.

Whatever culture you decide to create it will take a while to create it. Your culture might be fun based, success based, financial achievement based, client service based, team based – or all of the above. To change your culture will mean changing some of your people (who do not buy into the new culture) and it will mean summarizing it into written performance standards.

Your performance standards are how you want to people to act and behave. Your performance standards should be everywhere and everyone should have a copy of them with them at all times. You can incorporate your performance standards into your daily / weekly training or meeting program and you can incorporate them into career development and performance management.

My business is not perfect by any means (which one is?), however the consistent and positive comments we receive from clients regarding my team and team culture indicate that we do it better than most. To give you an insight into my service and success orientated culture, here is an in-depth look at my business where my team operates under 14 core performance standards and 6 core values.

We use these performance standards in training, performance management, induction, team meetings and of course, client / prospect interactions.

Nixon Advantage Client Service Performance Standards:

1. I lead by example.

What does that mean? It means that we practice what we preach. We have a massive range of content that we educate the profession on. We need to make sure we are using that for our business. That means that everyone needs to know our content. It means that if we are telling our clients to set and achieve goals then we should do the same. It means that if we are telling our clients to give great customer service, then our service should be even better than the clients'. It means that if we tell our clients that they should be involved in personal development and learning, then we should do more of it.

Our clients are the natural leaders of business – the trusted advisors. The trusted advisors should be running a better business than those that they advise. We are leading the accounting profession, which means that we should be running the best business out of the lot of them with the best people, the best processes, the best marketing, the best sales and the best logistical management. THE BEST.

2. I constantly raise the bar as we lead the accounting profession.

This is all about inspiring our clients.

- If we are running a better business than our clients then we will inspire them.
- If we are coming up with content and methods that are leading edge then we will inspire them.
- If we are listening (really listening) to our current clients successes and then re-telling those stories to other clients / prospects then we will inspire them.
- If we push the boundaries of what is possible then we will inspire them.
- If we develop ourselves personally and use the right language and communicate eloquently then we will inspire them.
- If we adopt 'better than best practice' finance, admin, marketing, sales and coaching methods then we will inspire them.
- If we challenge them then we will inspire them.

3. Clients will be completely delighted with what I do, and how I do it.

The end result of this standard is *'100% referenceable'*. That means if we had to roll out our client list, prospect list and anyone we have had contact with over the years (to an external party for due diligence for example) that they would say amazing things about the people they have dealt with and the experience they have had. It means that the 4 'easys' have been working to make it an unbelievable experience:

1. Easy to deal with (all things people & logistics).
2. Easy to understand (product / service).
3. Easy to buy (marketing / sales process).
4. Easy to implement (what they buy works).

4. I always maintain positive relationships.

Negativity is a cancer and toxic relationships never last. When we work with clients (internal and external) we are there to build a relationship – a professional and positive relationship. We are not building 'buddies for life' we are building 'clients for life'. To do that we must be really focussed on what we say, how we say it, when we say it, why we say it and most importantly how we say it.

We are in business; this is not a day care centre or a nice comfortable billeted homestay. We have a business to run and as such we must build relationships with our clients that are professional by nature and commercial by standing.

5. I greet and farewell everyone by name with eye contact and with a smile.

Here are some examples. If you answer the phone correctly with, "Welcome to Nixon Advantage this is [first name] [last name]," then the person on the other end of the phone will (in most cases) give you their full name. You can then bring up the database and see who you are speaking with and start a positive conversation. At any event do not be shy and wait for the person to come to you – go from behind the desk and extend your hand (to shake theirs) and say, 'Welcome to coachingclub / [name of seminar], I'm [first name], [last name].'

Continue to look people in the eye when they are speaking with you. It's a simple one but often overlooked. It shows you are interested and you are listening. On the phone smile – you can hear the smile! When you wrap up the call – leave it with something like, 'Thanks for the call [name], I'll be making that happen right away for you.'

6. If at fault, I will apologise and make restitution– right away.

What does that mean? Pretty much what it says, however the way you apologise can make a difference. Just writing, "I'm sorry" is probably not enough. You need some explanation around it.

With apologising it takes a big person to admit they are wrong. Most people act below the line and make excuses; they blame others and are in denial about the real situation. If you have made a mistake (and we all have) then admit it, make restitution somehow, apologise in a heartfelt way and then move on. The worst are the ones who deny that they have done wrong. Apologise to clients, to suppliers, to team members and alliance partners.

7. I demonstrate a positive 'can do' attitude at all times.

On a day-to-day basis you have a choice of operating **below the line** or **above the line**. Both will impact your thinking and personal results.

Operating below the line is...

- ☒ Thinking negatively about situations.
- ☒ Worrying about things that never eventuate.
- ☒ Blaming others for your actions.
- ☒ Not taking responsibility for your actions.
- ☒ Making excuses for your personal performance.
- ☒ Being in denial about what is really going on.
- ☒ Saying 'yes, but' to situations / ideas – yes, but that will never work.

Operating above the line is...

- ✓ Realising that there is a positive in every negative.
- ✓ Having a pleasant disposition every day.
- ✓ Taking responsibility.
- ✓ Being accountable – doing what you say you are going to do.
- ✓ Using the words "MUST", "WILL" and "COMMIT" on a daily basis.
- ✓ Having a high self-esteem problem.
- ✓ Believing that anything is possible.

Having a 'can do' attitude is about you being as awesome as you can be and delivering a client experience where you take responsibility and make it happen.

8. I focus on solutions to clients objectives.

To focus on clients' objectives you must first ask questions around what their objectives are. What their motivation is and what their problems are. People are motivated to do something different (whether in a marketing, sales or coaching role) because of a number of factors:

50% of the reasons why they will change:

- ✓ The clients' reasons as to why they should.
- ✓ The clients' motivation.
- ✓ The clients' objectives.
- ✓ The clients' benefits received.

40% of the reasons why they will change:

- ✓ The relationship they have with you.
- ✓ The credibility belief they have with you.
- ✓ The trust they have with you.
- ✓ The likeability of you.

10% of the reasons why they will change:

- ✓ The actual product they are buying.
- ✓ The actual process they will be going through.
- ✓ The actual content they will be using.
- ✓ The actual methodology that us used.

Spend time on finding out what the clients / prospects want and need and then build a closer relationship with them. Once you have that then you can recommend solutions to help them.

9. I am creative and innovative in my approach to helping our clients succeed.

The success of this business is predicated on the success of our clients. If we want to promote how good we are then we need to promote that fact via the success of our clients. First of all we MUST help our clients succeed. That means listening and flexibility.

If we are listening to our clients and what we are doing is not working, then let's change what we are doing. Flexibility is key. If the market tells us by complaint, resignation, murmur, rumour or inference then we must listen to that – and be BIG enough to do something different.

If we are really listening to our clients then we must promote the fact – via regular (minimum monthly) case studies, regular (monthly) tele-seminars, regular white papers and reports and stories, stories and more stories. The story you hear from one client can be used to help another client.

10. I always act with integrity, I respect others and I and use empowering conversation.

The way you act on a day-to-day basis is critical to your success and the businesses success. Are you acting in an integral way – doing what is right and just? Do you respect the person you are speaking with – will they one day be the next superstar of business? Do you use empowering and uplifting conversation – or is it negative and nasty?

Doing the right thing in any situation, respecting someone else's position, opinion or situation and speaking politely in an uplifting way...it's just good manners!

11. I always reply to all communication by the end of the same day that it was received.

What does that mean? It's basic courtesy and manners. If someone **internal** or **external** communicates with you and requests an answer then you answer it – on the same day. However, if someone emails you at 4pm on a Friday you may not have time to answer – so a quick, "I'll come back to you on Monday," will suffice. You've still answered on the same day.

Replying to communication includes: Emails, mail, fax, phone calls or SMS. It means that you do not have anything in your email inbox that has not been dealt with every day. Every day make sure you file, action, reply, or trash your emails – **every single day**. If you reply to communications every day, then you will be giving outstanding service and you will be known for promptness.

12. I will own any queries or complaints that I receive, and ensure they are addressed within the same business day that I receive them.

What does this mean? It means you do not pass the buck and say, 'That's not my job' and refuse to sort something out. Instead if you say: 'I am sorry to hear about that. Although I do not handle that myself I am going to go and speak with X and get back to you with a resolution'.

You then speak with the person who can resolve it, you communicate back to the person who had the issue and then you connect the 2 people to sort it out. A follow up call always helps as well. Do it all same day so the issue is sorted out. A complaint is an opportunity to shine and be awesome.

13. I always answer the telephone within 2 rings and with a smile and I always say Say, "Welcome to Nixon Advantage, this is [first name], [last name]."

What does that mean? It means that we have consistency in our process and we run to the phone if we need to. From the callers' point of view, there is nothing more annoying than a phone that rings and rings and rings. It comes across like 'they are arrogant and don't care'. If you answer the call on the first ring the caller does not have a chance to settle themself. If you answer it on the 3rd or more rings then the caller gets annoyed. When you hear 3 the caller hears 4.

If you answer with a smile the caller can 'hear' the smile. If you answer without a smile then they can 'hear' that as well. You never get a second chance to make a first impression.

The way you announce yourself is critical in this process. The **'this is'** indicates something important is about to happen. You do not say 'speaking' at the end of your name – of course you are speaking. You do not say 'may I help you' at the end of your name – that's what you're there to do.

Your full name is critical as well because the law of physiological reciprocity (what you give out you get back) kicks in when you announce yourself – they will tell you their full name. If you announce your full name and then pause the only response is their full name – in the majority of cases. You have stated your company and your name – they will (in the majority of cases) state their company and full name.

14. I am always 'on the stage' and act accordingly.

People on the stage speak correctly, dress correctly and act appropriately. People on the stage are aware of their presence and their actions. They are aware that a media critic may be in the audience and they always play 'full out' at every show. They are rarely 'off' and are always 'on'. Good stage performers use the proper vocabulary with everyone they meet. They do not use slang, drop their 'g's' (comin & goin) or talk down to people in demeaning ways.

They use correct phrases like 'good morning', 'certainly', 'I'll happy to' and 'it's my pleasure'. Every interaction with a person (team member, supplier, alliance or client) is a potential business transaction. Make it count by being 'on the stage' all the time.

15. I always live and demonstrate the company values of: Being ethical, courageous, caring, open-minded, practicing what we preach and fun.

✓ **Ethical**: *Doing the right things.* That means if we know someone is not suited to our business then we need to tell them. It means that if we owe money then we pay money – on time. It means that we give the right advice all the time. It means we should say 'no' if it's appropriate.

✓ **Courageous**: *Having the strength to be bold and stepping up.* This means you are not a 'shrinking violet'. If you want to say something then say it. If you believe in something then make it happen. It means you need to 'push back' if a prospect or client is giving you an unfair or hard time. It means you promote what you believe in. It means you go out of your comfort zone to make a difference.

✓ **Caring**: *Building genuine relationships.* It means that you follow our 'relationship enhancement' program. It means you are genuine in your approach and service. It means you make an effort to get to know all of your clients – they are all 'A' class clients. It means that all of our clients should be saying, 'I have a great relationship with the team at Nixon Advantage'.

✓ **Open-minded**. *Open to new ideas and change.* It means that you are flexible and enthusiastic about new ideas. It means that when an idea is presented you do not automatically say, 'yes, but' (and come up with a negative), instead you look to the positive and ask questions so the idea can be improved or removed. It means that if there is a proven 'better way' then be bold enough to change what you have been doing.

✓ **Practice What We Preach**. *Doing what we tell others to do.* That means if we promote something in writing, from a seminar stage, to a client and it is applicable to our business then we must do it. It means that if we are leading our clients and they are leading their clients then we should be running a better business than all of them. Not bigger, not more profitable – but better. Better marketing, better sales process, better logistical management, better relationship management, better systems, better leadership and the best team of people we can get.

✓ **Fun**. *Do what you love and love what you do.* That means that everyone should be in their 'happy place' doing a job that enriches their life. It means that every day there should be laughter and positive emotion. That means that interactions with our company (clients, suppliers, alliances and friends) should be fun. It means that clients tell us that they have fun at our events and meetings. It means that you should think of many ways to make the experience in dealing with us even more fun.

You need to develop your performance standards that suit your culture.

Getting Buy-In

One of the most common questions in relation to team members is getting them to 'buy-in' to your new ideas. Having your team right behind you as you conquer the world! Team buy-in is all about change management. The more aligned you are as a business the faster and easier you will be able reach your goals.

For a traditional accounting practice that has been operating the same way for a long period of time then (unless you change your entire team) change will take some time – but not as long as you think. However, what you will find is that many of your team members are just waiting for something exciting to happen.

With change and buy-in you have to remember a few things:

1. Your team (and your business) have been doing the 'old way' for many years.

2. The new way may seem to make sense but some of the team think the old way is not really broken - you are getting by doing what you are doing.

3. Change management is not a singular event – you constantly have to drive it.

So with that in mind here are some ideas you can do to change behaviour and get constant buy-in.

1. Search for the reasons **why** you want to change from a leadership level. You need to have the leadership team (other partners and/or key stakeholders) buy-into the change first, otherwise you have little hope of success. Alignment at the shareholder level is crucial to your success. The shareholders must have objectives that they are motivated by. If your shareholders are comfortable, not ambitious, have no goals and very happy with the status quo (and you are the opposite) then you will have some major difficulties. You may need to leave your current business or get some new shareholders! If you need to bring in some outside help to guide you through this, then do it.

2. Decide **what** it is you want to change. Do you want to change the entire business or just some tactical aspects like pricing up front instead of pricing in arrears? Make a list of the critical strategies that need attention and prioritise them. Get the list to be as short and succinct as possible. In my business we focus on 5 key priorities each quarter and then we have the number

1 priority that when implemented the rest follow. We have quarterly business priorities, CEO priorities, team priorities and individual priorities.

3. Decide **who** needs to change. Is the entire team involved or just a critical few. My advice is that the entire team should be involved with doing something.

4. Decide **when** you want to change. Too much change too fast can cause disruption. Spread the change out over a few years. Have a 10 year, 3 year, 1 year and 90 day plan.

5. Decide what the non-negotiable **rules** (e.g all jobs priced upfront, value pricing, proactive focus, client communication strategy) are from a leadership level. It's your business. You may not tell the team the rules just yet - you might need to have the team buy into the new rules.

6. Conduct **events** that show your team why they need to change. This could include regular training, seminars, client case studies, industry facts, internal testing, social proof of other firms who have been successful.

7. Always bring it back to **WIIFM** - what's in it for me! Your team are interested in a better working environment, their enjoyment, salary & benefits, fulfilling work, clients' success and career development.

8. Promote, promote, promote and don't give up. If you believe that change needs to happen and it is in the best interests of your business then be like a dog with a bone. If after constant coaching of your team they do not buy-in, then coach them out.

In response to a recent forum post by a new member on 'getting team buy-in' one of our most successful clients (David) wrote this excellent response.

This is by far the biggest challenge that you will face on your journey. We have been around coachingclub since day one and with up to 100 people to keep engaged, I have constantly been challenged with this question. I am sure that you have heard of the word chunking. Well we take the list of things to be done, break them down into chunks and then allocate the responsibility for implementation to accountants within the business. Not partners or managers but everyday accountants who are on the floor and at the coal-face. They would report their progress to me monthly and I would give them all the support they needed to implement the change.

I always found that getting the partners and managers to commit was the easy part because I dealt with them regularly. The best way to get everyone else involved was then to charge them with the responsibility of making it happen. Partners and managers have enough responsibility. I would run a competition to see who could implement things the best. At the end of a period (could be 6 months or whatever was appropriate) I would award a prize for the most successful person (and their group). This always ensured that things were happening as the drive was from the staff and the prize was always well sought after.

Buy-in is not a singular event. It takes time to change people's behaviour.

Implementing Anything

What's the point of coming up with an idea unless it is implemented? If the idea is worthy of the research, thinking, brainstorming and effort needed to crystallise it then don't you think it deserves to be implemented? Yet many good ideas are not implemented.

Implementation is relatively easy if you know how to implement anything. I learned how to implement projects through necessity.

In a former life, I was asked to be the General Manager at a small company that was in trouble. It had just come out of a disastrous merger and was making losses (a loss of $340K where normally it had a $1M profit), it had mounting debt ($1M cash debt instead of cash in the bank) and sales had declined by 50% to $3.4M. Technically it was insolvent, however the overseas parent company was propping it up with cash so it could pay its bills. Team morale was very low and the clients were not happy either. My job as the new GM was to fix it and re-build it. I gathered the team around (what was left of them) told them the brutal facts and between us we brainstormed 149 key projects that needed to be implemented. After 15 months we implemented 134 of the projects and the business looked completely different. Profit went from a loss of $340K to a profit of $2.5M. The $1M debt was paid back in full and sales went from $3.4M to $6.7M. The business was fixed up, rebuilt and it was then sold for many millions of dollars.

To grow a business or to turn one around, it takes focus and discipline. I used a 9 step process that I developed whilst turning that business around. Since then I have fine-tuned it and used it over and over again with many businesses and with many clients. I call it '**Lasercution**' – execution with laser focus.

1 - Motivation. As the GM I was very motivated. I had a 5% bonus riding on profit improvement over a certain figure. You must find your personal motivation and your team motivation. During the course of the turnaround I gave away around $100K in bonuses to the team as well as trips, vouchers and other rewards as an incentive or a job well done.

2- Buy-In. Once the brutal facts were uncovered (all of them) I asked who was in and who was out. I had some resignations – 5 in one day. That was OK because the new people I hired didn't know any different. The balance of the team was committed to making the business happen. I conducted 'team advance' sessions every quarter to re-plan, report and have fun. For more detail see 'getting buy-in' information in the proceeding pages.

3 - Planning. I asked the team what needed to be done to fix and re-build the business. We had an initial planning session and it was the team that came up with the project list of 149 – not me as the chief. These days I keep my business plan to 1 page (albeit A3 in size) that covers every aspect of my business. It is reviewed every week and implemented every day.

4 - Key Projects. Once we had the project list we put them into categories. For example: marketing, sales, logistics, finance, client service, products etc. Each project was categorised, prioritised, date bound and each one had a project leader who would be responsible for reporting on the success of the project.

5 - ON Time. Every week working ON time should be in your diary. This is the time that you are not interrupted so you can focus on important business development projects. The writing of this book is a great example. In total it will take about 100 hours to write and edit. I spread that time over a 3 month period with blocked out time in my diary. Each project leader needs ON time in their diary so they can focus on projects that are not associated with client delivery.

6 - Themes. Each quarter, a theme needs to be developed and rolled out to your team members. The theme for the quarter could be internal and/or external. An internal theme might be: clean up, buzz, blast off or systems. An external theme might be: client cash flow, client profit, client assets, client wealth. Have some fun with this and promote this to team members as well as clients.

7 - Visual Management. Once you have your projects, your themes, goals and plans, do not just hide them in a written report, file or spreadsheet. Get them out there in a visual format. Use whiteboards, colourful props, large thermometers for targets, ships bells, flip charts that stick to walls, even sticky notes on your computer to keep you reminded. My main team meeting room is called 'the situation room' where you would normally call it a 'board room'. Is it a boardroom or a bored room? I love the use of white boards for planning and visual management. It's very powerful to be constantly reminded, when you see it every day.

8 - Accountability. If each person has set their own targets and timeframes then they can be held accountable to those targets and timeframes. If you want someone to be accountable you have to give them control of what they are accountable of. I like to keep people accountable on a daily basis. We have a short (no more than 45 seconds per person on a stopwatch) daily stand up meeting at 10.10 every morning. We call it our 10@1010. Each person has to answer 3 questions: 1) What's up – what are you specifically doing today? 2) Daily metrics – what are your numbers or outcomes that you are focused on today? 3) Where are you stuck – do you need any help to keep you on track? On a weekly basis I run a full management meeting for management accountability (50 minutes) and then a monthly, quarterly and annual planning session as well. If people are consistently missing their targets then alternative solutions and coaching is provided or we find people who can meet their targets.

9 - Coaching. Ever since I turned the above-mentioned business around, I have been a big believer in coaching. I had a business coach to help me do it. The best athletes have a coach. The best business people have a coach. It is lonely in business and I believe every business person needs outside support to guide, keep on track, encourage and motivate them. I have used many forms of coaching over the years. I have used 'mastermind' groups where you informally meet with like- minded business people and keep each other accountable. I have hired personal coaches who just help me and I have been in 'group' coaching. For implementation, the most effective form of coaching is group-based coaching. The reason is, on a 'one on one' basis you can still get away with not implementing. Think of group coaching like a formal board of directors with a chairperson. When you have to turn up to 7 (or more) other business people AND a coach and report in, it becomes very embarrassing if you have not implemented what you said you were going to do. You are more motivated to achieve more when there is more accountability.

When you spend the time developing a plan, make sure you spend the time to implement it. As my friend Michael Sheargold says, "*The power of an idea is in its implementation!*"

9

Design Your Model – It's Yours!

Remember this. Your accounting firm is a <u>business</u> that you have bought into, inherited or started. It is not a job where you are told what to do. It is a business where you can call the shots. It is not your clients business, or your employees business – it's your business! And you can design your business anyway that suits you. There is no right or wrong model – it's what suits your ambition, your goals and your lifestyle. In this chapter I am going to explore 4 different models that you could adopt.

Does Solo Mean Bliss?

In some advisory industries being a complete solo (no employees) is a great business model. In the accounting business I am yet to meet a successful one who has no employees. The reason is that clients have many needs and you need the leverage of employees to help you out.

However, you can be a successful single-owner accounting business that has employees. This is often called the sole practitioner model. It can be lonely being a solo practitioner and it can have a lot of benefits as well. The biggest benefit I hear is that you have no one else (other partners) to argue with or convince. The sole practitioner model can be extremely profitable with the right leverage. I know of a sole practitioner accounting business that does $15M in revenue with a considerable profit!

The unprofitable sole practitioners are the ones that do not have much leverage (people to partner ratio) and the majority of the workload falls on the owner. These businesses are trying to be all things to all people and they will never get anywhere.

If you are going to be a single owner business then you need scale. If you want to have a reasonable lifestyle (time and money) then you need to have much more than $1M in revenue. The most successful sole practitioners I know have more than 10 people and have revenue of more than $2M.

Boutique and Niche

There is nothing wrong with being a boutique small business (by headcount) provided you get really focused on whom you are serving and what you are delivering to them.

You may choose an industry that you are passionate about and you can become an industry expert in that field. If you become an industry expert then you can charge higher fees and get very focused on your marketing and sales activity.

You may chose a niche service offering what you are passionate about. You can outsource many services these days to generalists if you decide to become a specialist. If you look at the medical community, the specialists are making more money than the generalists. The flip side to that is often the specialists are working very long (and sometimes odd) hours.

If you decide to be boutique and niche then stay that way. You can charge high fees for your unique expertise but you will not have a business that you can sell. Other than administration support, the business will heavily rely on you.

Getting Bigger

Most firms get bigger by osmosis. It just happens. They grow by people numbers, partner numbers, office space and the revenue certainly grows. But the profit per partner does not necessarily grow in line with the revenue percentage. It frequently goes backwards - or stays around the same.

If you decide to get bigger by headcount and shareholders then the critical thing you need to remember is leverage. Specifically leverage of people per partner. There is no point bringing in another equity partner if you are not planning on growing your revenue and profit dramatically.

Under the old practice model once a partnership gets to around $1M revenue per partner they think they must get another partner. It doesn't need to be like that. You'll end up with too many partners and not enough profitability.

In my view the leverage of people per partner needs to be well over 15 people before you entertain another full equity partner. You can certainly have employee shareholders who buy a small percentage of the firm but full equity partners – proceed with caution.

As you grow, one of the critical 'hires' that you need as you get larger is a full time Business Manager, someone who is running the day-to-day operations. This person will allow the leadership team to focus on client success. The right time to hire a business manager is when you are ready to grow. I have seen sole practitioners with 6 people have a full time business manager. I have also seen 40 person firms who do not have one (the partners share the load) and they do not grow.

You can grow your business to whatever size you want. As you do, make sure you focus on growing the revenue per person, the profit person and the profit per client.

Roll Up, Roll Up

The consolidation (public companies buying accounting firms) movement started in the late 1990's. There have been many spectacular failures and a few successes. By and large the accounting profession is a 'cottage industry', which has been run by technicians attempting to be business people. In every jurisdiction there are thousands of accounting firms with a limited future for the partners.

As your firm gets larger who are you going to sell it to? A consolidator is certainly a viable choice. They have scale, people to support you, broad range of services already developed, cash now, the ability to raise cash through the public sector and they provide a future for your team through employee share schemes and proper HR management. If you sell to a consolidator you will get a healthy price for your firm. Many consolidators will pay 4 and sometimes even up to 6 times EBIT after partners' salaries. Ideally your consideration will be in cash but even if it is in cash and tradable shares (and ideally you ride the share price) then that can work in your favour.

It sounds very attractive, so what's the downside? Other than the obvious of not getting a return on your shares or losing your firm because the consolidator mismanaged the business and went broke – I see only one potential disadvantage that will not suit everyone.

You will be an employee of a large corporation.

If you are okay with not being the master of your own destiny and not being an entrepreneur (you can still be an intraprenuer – an internal entrepreneur) then go for it. If you are planning on retiring (or getting out of the industry altogether) from your firm over the next few years then go for it.

Of course like any sale or purchase of a business do thorough due diligence and negotiate good terms for yourself.

The consolidation of accounting firms is here to stay. In fact, I think it will escalate. The value of an accounting business client base is increased with scale.

Your Ideal Business Life

Spend some quality time working out what you want your ideal business life to look like. Your business is not your entire life so don't let it consume you. As my friend Alan says, *'Your business is fuel for your life not the other way round.'*

If you decide to work 3 days per week then do that. If you decide to work remotely then do that. If you decide to have 10 weeks per year off then do that. If you decide to only come into your office on Mondays and Fridays then do that. If you decide to work on Saturdays and have Wednesdays off then do that. If you decide to only work with certain types of clients then do that. If you decide to do only certain types of work then do that. If you decide to not-run your businesses then do that. If you decide to have 100 people and 3 locations then do that. If you decide to incorporate business with pleasure by working on holidays then do that. If you decide to travel first class and 5 star then do that. If you decide to give money and time to charitable causes then do that. If you decide to earn over $1M per partner then do that.

There is no right or wrong model. It's what works best for you.

Whatever **result** you are looking for, then make the appropriate **decisions**, workout what **actions** need to happen – and just go and do that!

10

Changing the World

I am very excited about the accounting profession. It's a noble industry that has a general perception of being a bit boring, staid and dull. I disagree. I think if the business is run correctly it can be a fabulous business that provides an awesome lifestyle for everyone in it.

As the industry goes forward the role of technology will play an important part. The imagination of technology providers and broadband speeds are holding the industry back. I think social media will connect the clients of firms together like a concierge service – with the ability to find services quickly and deal with leading businesses. Technology will come into its own as real time (and extremely high quality) video training, support and business advice is delivered over the Internet through fixed and mobile devices.

The next partners coming through are a bit different from the current partners. Often called 'Generation Y' the current accountants working in firms are aged (at the time of writing) 20 – 35 years old. They are looking for faster career progression and a different lifestyle to you. Is your firm adapting fast enough to support this group?

I think networks of firms will play a crucial part in the success of an individual of a firm. Having like-minded (yet independent) firms working together on client projects and having the ability to 'bounce ideas' off each other will be the way of the future.

As a multi-disciplinary firm progresses it will be able to say 'yes' to any client situation because of the people hired within the firm or the access to knowledge from their network of firms. Because modern accounting businesses do not see themselves as competitors to other firms – they believe in growing the size of the pie rather than the size of the slice – they will share intellectual property (through knowledge factories) amongst themselves. The accounting firm of the future will operate more like a bureau service and marketing business and as such, building enduring client relationships will be even more important.

Why Accountants?

I get asked all the time why I chose accountants to work with. I think as I look back as to how I got started I have come to the realisation that accountants actually chose me. You know that I am not an accountant (nor will I ever be one) and you now know that I have forged a unique niche in the worldwide profession as a thought leader and entrepreneur.

After years of working with accountants I have come to understand my true purpose as to why I work with accountants. Here it is…

If I, and the people around me, can help accounting practices to become accounting businesses and during the process we help them to sort out their operations, client service, people, workflow management, marketing, sales, profit and cash flow then we can make a significant difference.

If we can also show those same accounting businesses how to offer value added services to their clients that help their clients with growth, profit, cash flow improvement, asset protection and wealth creation then we can make a significant difference.

If we can do that enough times with enough accounting firms then **we can change the world** – one business at a time. That's why. Get involved. Start a movement of improvement. Go to my websites to download hints, tips, articles, and sign up for newsletters and other free cool stuff.

Come with me as we change the world.

Enquiry Form

Please contact me regarding the following services:

- A Firm Financial Analysis is an introductory free 90 minute consultation used to uncover and highlight areas in your firm that would benefit from improving. These areas can include; improving cash flow, reducing WIP and debtor days, and increasing revenue and profit. This initial consultation is conducted over the phone & web with one our Performance Advisors. Although valued at $990 this service is complimentary.

- The 'Business Performance Review' will assist you in analysing your current performance and will then provide you with detailed recommendations on: 1. Where are you now, 2. What is possible, 3. How do you rate? It is a content rich, face-to-face planning / strategy session. The program is highly customised to focus specifically on the areas most relevant to your business.

- Coachingclub membership will keep you accountable to your objectives, KPIs and projects. You will be matched with 7 other firms who are on a similar development path to you. You will learn from the other firms in your club and will be held accountable by a highly trained coach.

- Being a member of the Proactive Accountants Network is the only network of proactive accountants in the world. It is a way to differentiate your firm from your competitors. You will connect with like minded firms in a formal network, receive unique branding and marketing material and have the ability to share people and content with other firms around the globe.

- Private consulting, training or speaking. If you are a larger firm who needs one on one help or you need a speaker at your next conference then we have expert trainers and speakers (including Rob) who can inspire, assist and teach.

Your contact details:

Name:_____   Firm name:_____

Your position:_____   No. Partners: _____ Team size: _____

Address: _____

Country: _____   Website: _____

Phone:_____   E-mail:_____

FAX, EMAIL OR POST THIS FORM TO;
ROB NIXON c/o NIXON ADVANTAGE
11/65 JAMES STREET, FORTITUDE VALLEY, QLD 4006 AUSTRALIA
 P +61 7 3607 6600   F +61 7 3036 6153
info@nixonadvantage.com   www.nixonadvantage.com

CPSIA information can be obtained at www.ICGtesting.com
Printed in the USA
BVOW01s0321220916

462823BV00011B/226/P

9 781921 787355